OTHER BOO

How High...

Eloquence

How Legendary Leaders Speak

Influential Leadership

Public Speaking Mastery

The 7 Keys to Confidence

Trust is Power

Influence

Decoding Human Nature

The Psychology of Persuasion

How Visionaries Speak

The Eloquent Leader

The Language of Leadership

The Psychology of Communication

The Charisma Code

Available on Amazon

Claim These Free Resources that Will Help You Unleash the Power of Your Words and Speak with Confidence. Visit www.speakforsuccesshub.com/toolkit for Access.

18 Free PDF Resources

30 Free Video Lessons

2 Free Workbooks

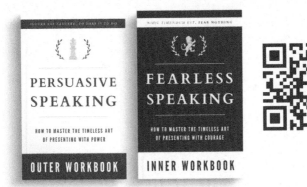

Claim These Free Resources that Will Help You Unleash the Power of Your Words and Speak with Confidence. Visit www.speakforsuccesshub.com/toolkit for Access.

18 Free PDF Resources

12 Iron Rules for Captivating Story, 21 Speeches that Changed the World, 341-Point Influence Checklist, 143 Persuasive Cognitive Biases, 17 Ways to Think On Your Feet, 18 Lies About Speaking Well, 137 Deadly Logical Fallacies, 12 Iron Rules For Captivating Slides, 371 Words that Persuade, 63 Truths of Speaking Well, 27 Laws of Empathy, 21 Secrets of Legendary Speeches, 19 Scripts that Persuade, 12 Iron Rules For Captivating Speech, 33 Laws of Charisma, 11 Influence Formulas, 219-Point Speech-Writing Checklist, 21 Eloquence Formulas

30 Free Video Lessons

We'll send you one free video lesson every day for 30 days, written and recorded by Peter D. Andrei. Days 1-10 cover authenticity, the prerequisite to confidence and persuasive power. Days 11-20 cover building self-belief and defeating communication anxiety. Days 21-30 cover how to speak with impact and influence, ensuring your words change minds instead of falling flat. Authenticity, self-belief, and impact – this course helps you master three components of confidence, turning even the most high-stakes presentations from obstacles into opportunities.

2 Free Workbooks

We'll send you two free workbooks, including long-lost excerpts by Dale Carnegie, the mega-bestselling author of *How to Win Friends and Influence People* (5,000,000 copies sold). *Fearless Speaking* guides you in the proven principles of mastering your inner game as a speaker. *Persuasive Speaking* guides you in the time-tested tactics of mastering your outer game by maximizing the power of your words. All of these resources complement the Speak for Success collection.

ELOQUENCE

THE HIDDEN SECRET OF WORDS THAT
CHANGE THE WORLD

Peter Andrei

ELOQUENCE

SPEAK FOR SUCCESS COLLECTION BOOK

II

SPEAK
TRUTH
WELL
PRESS

A SUBSIDIARY OF SPEAK TRUTH WELL LLC
800 Boylston Street
Boston, MA 02199

SPEAK
TRUTH
WELL LLC

SPEAK FOR SUCCESS COLLECTION

Printed in the United States of America
40 39 38 37 36 35 34 33 32 31

While the author has made every effort to provide accurate internet addresses at the time of publication, neither the publisher nor the author assumes any responsibility for errors, or for changes that occur after publication. Further, the publisher does not have any control over and does not assume any responsibility for author or third-party websites or their content.

www.speakforsuccesshub.com/toolkit

FREE RESOURCES FOR OUR READERS

We believe in using the power of the internet to go above and beyond for our readers. That's why we created the free communication toolkit: 18 free PDF resources, 30 free video lessons, and even 2 free workbooks, including long-lost excerpts by Dale Carnegie, the mega-bestselling author of *How to Win Friends and Influence People.* (The workbooks help you put the most powerful strategies into action).

We know you're busy. That's why we designed these resources to be accessible, easy, and quick. Each PDF resource takes just 5 minutes to read or use. Each video lesson is only 5 minutes long. And in the workbooks, we bolded the key ideas throughout, so skimming them takes only 10 minutes each.

Why give so much away? For three reasons: we're grateful for you, it's useful content, and we want to go above and beyond. Questions? Feel free to email Peter directly at pandreibusiness@gmail.com.

www.speakforsuccesshub.com/toolkit

WHY DOES THIS HELP YOU?

I

The PDF resources cover topics like storytelling, logic, cognitive biases, empathy, charisma, and more. You can dig deeper into the specific topics that interest you most.

II

Many of the PDF resources are checklists, scripts, example-compilations, and formula-books. With these practical, step-by-step tools, you can quickly create messages that work.

III

With these free resources, you can supplement your reading of this book. You can find more specific guidance on the areas of communication you need to improve the most.

IV

The two workbooks offer practical and actionable guidance for speaking with complete confidence (*Fearless Speaking*) and irresistible persuasive power (*Persuasive Speaking*).

V

You can even learn from your phone with the free PDFs and the free video lessons, to develop your skills faster. The 30-lesson course reveals the secrets of building confidence.

VI

You are reading this because you want to improve your communication. These resources take you to the next level, helping you learn how to speak with power, impact, and confidence. We hope these resources make a difference. They are available here:

www.speakforsuccesshub.com/toolkit

From the desk of Peter Andrei
Speak Truth Well LLC
800 Boylston Street
Boston, MA 02199
pandreibusiness@gmail.com

May 15, 2021

What is Our Mission?

To whom it may concern:

The Wall Street Journal reports that public speaking is the world's biggest fear – bigger than being hit by a car. According to Columbia University, this pervasive, powerful, common phobia can reduce someone's salary by 10% or more. It can reduce someone's chances of graduating college by 10% and cut their chances of attaining a managerial or leadership position at work by 15%.

If weak presentation kills your good ideas, it kills your career. If weak communication turns every negotiation, meeting, pitch, speech, presentation, discussion, and interview into an obstacle (instead of an opportunity), it slows your progress. And if weak communication slows your progress, it tears a gaping hole in your confidence – which halts your progress.

Words can change the world. They can improve your station in life, lifting you forward and upward to higher and higher successes. But they have to be strong words spoken well: rarities in a world where most people fail to connect, engage, and persuade; fail to answer the question "why should we care about this?"; fail to impact, inspire, and influence; and, in doing so, fail to be all they could be.

Now zoom out. Multiply this dynamic by one thousand; one million; one billion. The individual struggle morphs into a problem for our communities, our countries, our world. Imagine the many millions of paradigm-shattering, life-changing, life-saving ideas that never saw the light of day. Imagine how many brilliant convictions were sunk in the shipyard. Imagine all that could have been that failed to be.

Speak Truth Well LLC solves this problem by teaching ambitious professionals how to turn communication from an obstacle into an engine: a tool for converting "what could be" into "what is." There is no upper limit: inexperienced speakers can become self-assured and impactful; veteran speakers can master the skill by learning advanced strategies; masters can learn how to outperform their former selves.

We achieve our mission by producing the best publications, articles, books, video courses, and coaching programs available on public speaking and communication, and at non-prohibitive prices. This combination of quality and accessibility has allowed Speak Truth Well to serve over 70,000 customers in its year of launch alone (2021). Grateful as we are, we hope to one day serve millions.

Dedicated to your success,

Peter Andrei
President of Speak Truth Well LLC
pandreibusiness@gmail.com

PROLOGUE:

This three-part prologue reveals my story, my work, and the practical and ethical principles of communication. It is not a mere introduction. It will help you get more out of the book. It is a preface to the entire 15-book Speak for Success collection. It will show you how to use the information with ease, confidence, and fluency, and how to get better results faster. If you would like to skip this, flip to page 50, or read only the parts of interest.

I

II

III

I

MY STORY AND THE STORY OF THIS COLLECTION

how I discovered the hidden key to successful communication, public speaking, influence, and persuasion (by reflecting on a painful failure)

HOW TO GAIN AN UNFAIR ADVANTAGE IN YOUR CAREER, BUSINESS, AND LIFE BY MASTERING THE POWER OF YOUR WORDS

I WAS SITTING IN MY OFFICE, TAPPING A PEN against my small wooden desk. My breaths were jagged, shallow, and rapid. My hands were shaking. I glanced at the clock: 11:31 PM. "I'm not ready." Have you ever had that thought?

I had to speak in front of 200 people the next morning. I had to convince them to put faith in my idea. But I was terrified, attacked by nameless, unreasoning, and unjustified terror which killed my ability to think straight, believe in myself, and get the job done.

Do you know the feeling?

After a sleepless night, the day came. I rose, wobbling on my tired legs. My head felt like it was filled with cotton candy. I couldn't direct my train of thoughts. A rushing waterfall of unhinged, self-destructive, and meaningless musings filled my head with an uncompromising cacophony of anxious, ricocheting nonsense.

"Call in sick."

"You're going to embarrass yourself."

"You're not ready."

I put on my favorite blue suit – my "lucky suit" – and my oversized blue-gold wristwatch; my "lucky" wristwatch.

"You're definitely not ready."

"That tie is ugly."

"You can't do this."

The rest went how you would expect. I drank coffee. Got in my car. Drove. Arrived. Waited. Waited. Waited. Spoke. Did poorly. Rushed back to my seat. Waited. Waited. Waited. Got in my car. Drove. Arrived home. Sat back in my wooden seat where I accurately predicted "I'm not ready" the night before.

Relieved it was over but disappointed with my performance, I placed a sheet of paper on the desk. I wrote "MY PROBLEMS" at the top, and under that, my prompt for the evening: "What did I do so badly? Why did everything feel so off? Why did the speech fail?"

"You stood in front of 200 people and looked at... a piece of paper, not unlike this one. What the hell were you thinking? You're not fooling anyone by reading a sentence and then looking up at them as you say it out loud. They know you're reading a manuscript, and they know what that means. You are unsure of yourself. You are unsure of your message. You are unprepared. Next: Why did you speak in that odd, low, monotone voice? That sounded like nails on a chalkboard. And it was inauthentic. Next: Why did you open by talking about yourself? Also, you're not particularly funny. No more jokes. And what was the structure of the speech? It had no structure. That, I feel, is probably a pretty big problem."

I believed in my idea, and I wanted to get it across. Of course, I wanted the tangible markers of a successful speech. I wanted action. I wanted the speech to change something in the real world. But my motivations were deeper than that. I wanted to see people "click" and come on board my way of thinking. I wanted to captivate the audience. I wanted to speak with an engaging, impactful voice, drawing the audience in, not repelling them. I wanted them to remember my message and to remember me. I wanted to feel, for just a moment, the thrill of power. But not the petty, forceful power of tyrants and dictators; the justified power – the earned power – of having a good idea and conveying it well; the power of Martin Luther King and John F. Kennedy; a power harnessed in service of a valuable idea, not the personal privilege of the speaker. And I wanted confidence: the quiet strength that comes from knowing your words don't stand in your way, but propel you and the ideas you care about to glorious new mountaintops.

Instead, I stood before the audience, essentially powerless. I spoke for 20 painful minutes – painful for them and for me – and then sat down. I barely made a dent in anyone's consciousness. I generated no excitement. Self-doubt draped its cold embrace over me. Anxiety built a wall between "what I am" and "what I could be."

I had tried so many different solutions. I read countless books on effective communication, asked countless effective communicators for their advice, and consumed countless courses on powerful public speaking. Nothing worked. All the "solutions" that didn't really solve my problem had one thing in common: they treated communication as an abstract art form. They were filled with vague, abstract pieces of advice like "think positive thoughts" and "be yourself." They confused me more than anything else. Instead of illuminating the secrets I had been looking for, they shrouded the elusive but indispensable skill of powerful speaking in uncertainty.

I knew I had to master communication. I knew that the world's most successful people are all great communicators. I knew that effective communication is the bridge between "what I have" and "what I want," or at least an essential part of that bridge. I knew that without effective communication – without the ability to influence, inspire, captivate, and move – I would be all but powerless.

I knew that the person who can speak up but doesn't is no better off than the person who can't speak at all. I heard a wise man say "If you can think and speak and write, you are absolutely deadly. Nothing can get in your way." I heard another wise man say "Speech is power: speech is to persuade, to convert, to compel. It is to bring another out of his bad sense into your good sense." I heard a renowned psychologist say "If you look at people who are remarkably successful across life, there's various reasons. But one of them is that they're unbelievably good at articulating what they're aiming at and strategizing and negotiating and enticing people with a vision forward. Get your words together... that makes you unstoppable. If you are an effective writer and speaker and communicator, you have all the authority and competence that there is."

When I worked in the Massachusetts State House for the Department of Public Safety and Homeland Security, I had the opportunity to speak with countless senators, state representatives, CEOs, and other successful people. In our conversations, however brief, I always asked the same question: "What are the ingredients of your success? What got you where you are?" 100% of them said effective communication. There was not one who said anything else. No matter their field – whether they were entrepreneurs, FBI agents, political leaders, business leaders, or multimillionaire donors – they all pointed to one skill: the ability to convey powerful words in powerful ways. Zero exceptions.

Can you believe it? It still astonishes me.

My problem, and I bet this may be your obstacle as well, was that most of the advice I consumed on this critical skill barely scratched the surface. Sure, it didn't make matters worse, and it certainly offered some improvement, but only in inches when I needed progress in miles. If I stuck with the mainstream public speaking advice, I knew I wouldn't unleash the power of my words. And if I didn't do that, I knew I would always accomplish much less than I could. I knew I would suffocate my own potential. I knew I would feel a rush of crippling anxiety every time I was asked to give a presentation. I knew I would live a life of less fulfillment, less success, less achievement, more frustration, more difficulty, and more anxiety. I knew my words would never become all they could be, which means that I would never become all I could be.

To make matters worse, the mainstream advice – which is not wrong, but simply not deep enough – is everywhere. Almost every article, book, or course published on this subject falls into the mainstream category. And to make matters worse, it's almost impossible to know that until you've spent your hard-earned money and scarce time with the resource. And even then, you might just shrug, and assume that shallow, abstract advice is all there is to the "art" of public speaking. As far as I'm concerned, this is a travesty.

I kept writing. "It felt like there was no real motive; no real impulse to action. Why did they need to act? You didn't tell them. What would happen if they didn't? You didn't tell them that either. Also, you tried too hard to put on a formal façade; you spoke in strange, twisted ways. It didn't sound sophisticated. And your mental game was totally off. You let your mind fill with destructive, doubtful, self-defeating thoughts. And your preparation was totally backward. It did more to set bad habits in stone than it did to set you up for success. And you tried to build suspense at one point but revealed the final point way too early, ruining the effect."

I went on and on until I had a stack of papers filled with problems. "That's no good," I thought. I needed solutions. Everything else I tried failed. But I had one more idea: "I remember reading a great speech. What was it? Oh yeah, that's right: JFK's inaugural address. Let me go pull it up and see why it was so powerful." And that's when everything changed.

I grabbed another sheet of paper. I opened JFK's inaugural address on my laptop. I started reading. Observing. Analyzing.

Reverse-engineering. I started writing down what I saw. Why did it work? Why was it powerful? I was like an archaeologist, digging through his speech for the secrets of powerful communication. I got more and more excited as I kept going. It was late at night, but the shocking and invaluable discoveries I was making gave me a burst of energy. It felt like JFK – one of the most powerful and effective speakers of all time – was coaching me in his rhetorical secrets, showing me how to influence an audience, draw them into my narrative, and find words that get results.

"Oh, so that's how you grab attention."

"Aha! So, if I tell them this, they will see why it matters."

"Fascinating – I can apply this same structure to my speech."

Around 3:00 in the morning, an epiphany hit me like a ton of bricks. That night, a new paradigm was born. A new opportunity emerged for all those who want to unleash the unstoppable power of their words. This new opportunity changed everything for me and eventually, tens of thousands of others. It is now my mission to bring it to millions, so that good people know what they need to know to use their words to achieve their dreams and improve the world.

Want to hear the epiphany?

The mainstream approach: Communication is an art form. It is unlike those dry, boring, "academic" subjects. There are no formulas. There are no patterns. It's all about thinking positive thoughts, faking confidence, and making eye contact. Some people are naturally gifted speakers. For others, the highest skill level they can attain is "not horrible."

The consequences of the mainstream approach: Advice that barely scratches the surface of the power of words. Advice that touches only the tip of the tip of the iceberg. A limited body of knowledge that blinds itself to thousands of hidden, little-known communication strategies that carry immense power; that blinds itself to 95% of what great communication really is. Self-limiting dogmas about who can do what, and how great communicators become great. Half the progress in twice the time, and everything that entails: missed opportunities, unnecessary and preventable frustration and anxiety, and confusion about what to say and how to say it. How do I know? Because I've been there. It's not pretty.

My epiphany, the new Speak for Success paradigm: Communication is as much a science as it is an art. You can study words that changed the world, uncover the hidden secrets of their power, and apply these proven principles to your own message. You can discover precisely what made great communicators great and adopt the same strategies. You can do this without being untrue to yourself or flatly imitating others. In fact, you can do this while being truer to yourself and more original than you ever have been before. Communication is not unpredictable, wishy-washy, or abstract. You can apply predictable processes and principles to reach your goals and get results. You can pick and choose from thousands of little-known speaking strategies, combining your favorite to create a unique communication approach that suits you perfectly. You can effortlessly use the same tactics of the world's most transformational leaders and speakers, and do so automatically, by default, without even thinking about it, as a matter of effortless habit. That's power.

The benefits of the Speak for Success paradigm: Less confusion. More confidence. Less frustration. More clarity. Less anxiety. More courage. You understand the whole iceberg of effective communication. As a result, your words captivate others. You draw them into a persuasive narrative, effortlessly linking your desires and their motives. You know exactly what to say. You know exactly how to say it. You know exactly how to keep your head clear; you are a master of the mental game. Your words can move mountains. Your words are the most powerful tools in your arsenal, and you use them to seize opportunities, move your mission forward, and make the world a better place. Simply put, you speak for success.

Fast forward a few years.

I was sitting in my office at my small wooden desk. My breaths were deep, slow, and steady. My entire being – mind, body, soul – was poised and focused. I set my speech manuscript to the side. I glanced at the clock: 12:01 AM. "Let's go. I'm ready."

I had to speak in front of 200 people the next morning. I had to convince them to put faith in my idea. And I was thrilled, filled with genuine gratitude at the opportunity to do what I love: get up in front of a crowd, think clearly, speak well, and get the job done.

I slept deeply. I dreamt vividly. I saw myself giving the speech. I saw myself victorious, in every sense of the word. I heard applause. I saw their facial expressions. I rose. My head was clear. My mental game was pristine. My mind was an ally, not an obstacle.

"This is going to be fun."

"I'll do my best, and whatever happens, happens."

"I'm so lucky that I get to do this again."

I put on my lucky outfit: the blue suit and the blue-gold watch.

"Remember the principles. They work."

"You developed a great plan last night. It's a winner."

"I can't wait."

The rest went how you would expect. I ate breakfast. Got in my car. Drove. Arrived. Waited. Waited. Waited. Spoke. Succeeded. Walked back to my seat. Waited. Waited. Waited. Got in my car. Drove. Arrived home. Sat back in my wooden seat where I accurately predicted "I'm ready" the night before.

I got my idea across perfectly. My message succeeded: it motivated action and created real-world change. I saw people "click" when I hit the rhetorical peak of my speech. I saw them leaning forward, totally hushed, completely absorbed. I applied the proven principles of engaging and impactful vocal modulation. I knew they would remember me and my message; I engineered my words to be memorable. I felt the thrilling power of giving a great speech. I felt the quiet confidence of knowing that my words carried weight; that they could win hearts, change minds, and help me reach the heights of my potential. I tore off the cold embrace of self-doubt. I defeated communication anxiety and broke down the wall between "what I am" and "what I could be."

Disappointed it was over but pleased with my performance, I placed a sheet of paper on the desk. I wrote "Speak Truth Well" and started planning what would become my business.

To date, we have helped tens of thousands of people gain an unfair advantage in their career, business, and life by unleashing the power of their words. And they experienced the exact same transformation I experienced when they applied the system.

If you tried to master communication before but haven't gotten the results you wanted, it's because of the mainstream approach; an approach that tells you "smiling at the audience" and "making eye contact" is all you need to know to speak well. That's not exactly a malicious lie – they don't know any better – but it is completely incorrect and severely harmful.

If you've been concerned that you won't be able to become a vastly more effective and confident communicator, I want to put those fears to rest. I felt the same way. The people I work with felt the same way. We just needed the right system. One public speaking book written by the director of a popular public speaking forum – I won't name names – wants you to believe that there are "nine public speaking secrets of the world's top minds." Wrong: There are many more than nine. If you feel that anyone who would boil down communication to just nine secrets is either missing something or holding it back, you're right. And the alternative is a much more comprehensive and powerful system. It's a system that gave me and everyone I worked with the transformation we were looking for.

Want to Talk? Email Me:

PANDREIBUSINESS@GMAIL.COM

This is My Personal Email.
I Read Every Message and
Respond in Under 12 Hours.

Visit Our Digital Headquarters:

WWW.SPEAKFORSUCCESSHUB.COM

See All Our Free Resources,
Books, Courses, and Services.

II

THE 15-BOOK SPEAK FOR SUCCESS COLLECTION

confidence, leadership, charisma, influence, public speaking, eloquence, human nature, credibility – it's all here, in a unified collection

MASTER EVERY ASPECT OF COMMUNICATION

T HE BESTSELLING SPEAK FOR SUCCESS COLLECTION covers every aspect of communication. Each book in the collection includes diagrams that visualize the essential principles, chapter summaries that remind you of the main ideas, and checklists of the action items in each section, all designed to help you consult the set as a reference.

This series is a cohesive, comprehensive set. After writing the first book, I realized how much information I couldn't fit into it. I wrote the second. After writing the second, the same thing happened. I wrote the third. The pattern continued. As of this writing, there are fifteen books in the collection. After writing each book, I felt called to write another. It is the ultimate communication encyclopedia.

Aside from a small amount of necessary overlap on the basics, each book is a distinct unit that focuses on an entirely new set of principles, strategies, and communication secrets. For example, *Eloquence* reveals the secrets of language that sounds good; *Trust is Power* reveals the secrets of speaking with credibility; *Public Speaking Mastery* reveals a blueprint for delivering speeches.

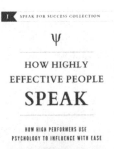

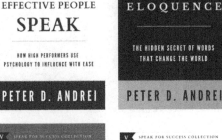

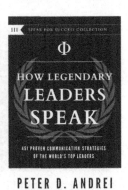

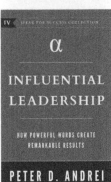

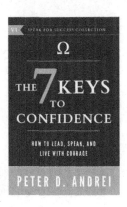

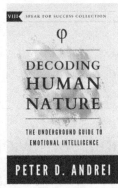

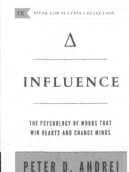

"The most complete and comprehensive collection of communication wisdom ever compiled." – Amazon Customer

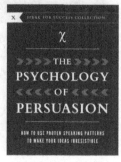
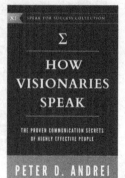
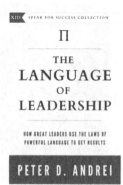
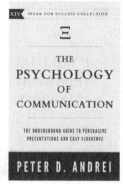

"I love the diagrams and summary checklists. I have all 15 on my shelf, and regularly refer back to them." – Amazon Customer

You Can Learn More Here:

www.speakforsuccesshub.com/series

................................A Brief Overview..................................

- I wrote *How Highly Effective People Speak* to reveal the hidden patterns in the words of the world's most successful and powerful communicators, so that you can adopt the same tactics and speak with the same impact and influence.

- I wrote *Eloquence* to uncover the formulas of beautiful, moving, captivating, and powerful words, so that you can use these exact same step-by-step structures to quickly make your language electrifying, charismatic, and eloquent.

- I wrote *How Legendary Leaders Speak* to illuminate the little-known five-step communication process the top leaders of the past 500 years all used to spread their message, so that you can use it to empower your ideas and get results.

- I wrote *Influential Leadership* to expose the differences between force and power and to show how great leaders use the secrets of irresistible influence to develop gentle power, so that you can move forward and lead with ease.

- I wrote *Public Speaking Mastery* to shatter the myths and expose the harmful advice about public speaking, and to offer a proven, step-by-step framework for speaking well, so that you can always speak with certainty and confidence.

- I wrote *The 7 Keys to Confidence* to bring to light the ancient 4,000-year-old secrets I used to master the mental game and speak in front of hundreds without a second of self-doubt or anxiety, so that you can feel the same freedom.

- I wrote *Trust is Power* to divulge how popular leaders and career communicators earn our trust, speak with credibility, and use this to rise to new heights of power, so that you can do the same thing to advance your purpose and mission.

- I wrote *Decoding Human Nature* to answer the critical question "what do people want?" and reveal how to use this knowledge to develop unparalleled influence, so that people adopt your idea, agree with your position, and support you.

- I wrote *Influence* to unearth another little-known five-step process for winning hearts and changing minds, so that you can know with certainty that your message will persuade people, draw support, and motivate enthusiastic action.

- I wrote *The Psychology of Persuasion* to completely and fully unveil everything about the psychology behind "Yes, I love it! What's the next step?" so that you can use easy step-by-step speaking formulas that get people to say exactly that.

- I wrote *How Visionaries Speak* to debunk common lies about effective communication that hold you back and weaken your words, so that you can boldly share your ideas without accidentally sabotaging your own message.

- I wrote *The Eloquent Leader* to disclose the ten steps to communicating with power and persuasion, so that you don't miss any of the steps and fail to connect, captivate, influence, and inspire in a crucial high-stakes moment.

- I wrote *The Language of Leadership* to unpack the unique, hidden-in-plain-sight secrets of how presidents and world-leaders build movements with the laws of powerful language, so that you use them to propel yourself forward.

- I wrote *The Psychology of Communication* to break the news that most presentations succeed or fail in the first thirty seconds and to reveal proven, step-by-step formulas that grab, hold, and direct attention, so that yours succeeds.

- I wrote *The Charisma Code* to shatter the myths and lies about charisma and reveal its nature as a concrete skill you can master with proven strategies, so that people remember you, your message, and how you electrified the room.

- **Learn more: www.speakforsuccesshub.com/series**

III

PRACTICAL TACTICS AND ETHICAL PRINCIPLES

how to easily put complex strategies into action and how to use the power of words to improve the world in an ethical and effective way

MOST COMMUNICATION BOOKS

HAVE YOU READ ANOTHER BOOK ON COMMUNICATION? If you have, let me remind you what you probably learned. And if you haven't, let me briefly spoil 95% of them. "Prepare. Smile. Dress to impress. Keep it simple. Overcome your fears. Speak from the heart. Be authentic. Show them why you care. Speak in terms of their interests. To defeat anxiety, know your stuff. Emotion persuades, not logic. Speak with confidence. Truth sells. And respect is returned."

There you have it. That is most of what you learn in most communication books. None of it is wrong. None of it is misleading. Those ideas are true and valuable. But they are not enough. They are only the absolute basics. And my job is to offer you much more.

Einstein said that "if you can't explain it in a sentence, you don't know it well enough." He also told us to "make it as simple as possible, but no simpler." You, as a communicator, must satisfy both of these maxims, one warning against the dangers of excess complexity, and one warning against the dangers of excess simplicity.

And I, as someone who communicates about communication in my books, courses, and coaching, must do the same.

THE SPEAK FOR SUCCESS SYSTEM

The Speak for Success system makes communication as simple as possible. Other communication paradigms make it even simpler. Naturally, this means our system is more complex. This is an unavoidable consequence of treating communication as a deep and concrete science instead of a shallow and abstract art. If you don't dive into learning communication at all, you miss out. I'm sure you agree with that. But if you don't dive *deep*, you still miss out.

THE FOUR QUADRANTS OF COMMUNICATION

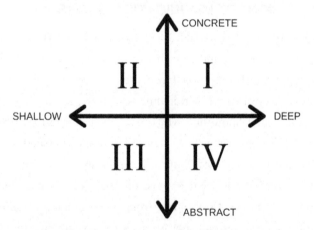

FIGURE VIII: There are four predominant views of communication (whether it takes the form of public speaking, negotiation, writing, or debating is irrelevant). The first view is that communication is concrete and deep. The second view is that communication is concrete and shallow. The third view is that communication is shallow and abstract. The fourth view is that communication is deep and abstract.

WHAT IS COMMUNICATION?

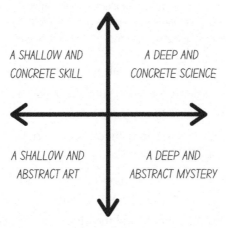

FIGURE VII: The first view treats communication as a science: "There are concrete formulas, rules, principles, and strategies, and they go very deep." The second view treats it as a skill: "Yes, there are concrete formulas, rules, and strategies, but they don't go very deep." The third view treats it as an art: "Rules? Formulas? It's not that complicated. Just smile and think positive thoughts." The fourth view treats it as a mystery: "How are some people such effective communicators? I will never know…"

WHERE WE STAND ON THE QUESTION

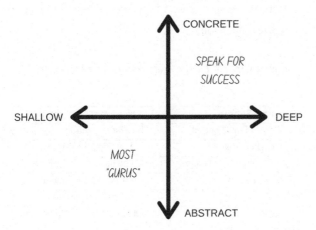

FIGURE VI: Speak for Success takes the view that communication is a deep and concrete science. (And by "takes the view," I mean "has discovered.") Most other communication writers, thought-leaders, public speaking coaches, and individuals and organizations in this niche treat communication as a shallow and abstract art.

This doesn't mean the Speak for Success system neglects the basics. It only means it goes far beyond the basics, and that it doesn't turn simple ideas into 200 pages of filler. It also doesn't mean that the Speak for Success system is unnecessarily complex. It is as simple as it can possibly be.

In this book, and in the other books of the Speak for Success collection, you'll find simple pieces of advice, easy formulas, and straightforward rules. You'll find theories, strategies, tactics, mental models, and principles. None of this should pose a challenge. But you'll also find advanced and complicated strategies. These might.

What is the purpose of the guide on the top of the next page? To reveal the methods that make advanced strategies easy. When you use the tactics revealed in this guide, the difficulty of using the advanced strategies drops dramatically. They empower you to use complicated and unfamiliar persuasive strategies with ease. If the 15-book Speak for Success collection is a complete encyclopedia of communication, to be used like a handbook, then this guide is a handbook for the handbook.

A SAMPLING OF EASY AND HARD STRATEGIES

Easy and Simple	Hard and Complicated
Use Four-Corner Eye Contact	The Fluency-Magnitude Matrix
Appeal to Their Values	The VPB Triad
Describe the Problem You Solve	The Illusory Truth Effect
Use Open Body Language	Percussive Rhythm
Tell a Quick Story	Alliterative Flow
Appeal to Emotion	Stacking and Layering Structures
Project Your Voice	The Declaratory Cascade
Keep it as Simple as Possible	Alternating Semantic Sentiments

THE PRACTICAL TACTICS

ECOGNIZE THAT, WITH PRACTICE, YOU can use any strategy extemporaneously. Some people can instantly use even the most complex strategies in the Speak for Success collection after reading them just once. They are usually experienced communicators, often with competitive experience. This is not an expectation, but a possibility, and with practice, a probability.

CREATE A COMMUNICATION PLAN. Professional communication often follows a strategic plan. Put these techniques into your plan. Following an effective plan is not harder than following an ineffective one. Marshall your arguments. Marshall your rhetoric. Stack the deck. Know what you know, and how to say it.

DESIGN AN MVP. If you are speaking on short notice, you can create a "minimum viable plan." This can be a few sentences on a notecard jotted down five minutes before speaking. The same principle of formal communication plans applies: While advanced strategies may overburden you if you attempt them in an impromptu setting, putting them into a plan makes them easy.

MASTER YOUR RHETORICAL STACK. Master one difficult strategy. Master another one. Combine them. Master a third. Build out a "rhetorical stack" of ten strategies you can use fluently, in impromptu or extemporaneous communication. Pick strategies that come fluently to you and that complement each other.

PRACTICE THEM TO FLUENCY. I coach a client who approached me and said he wants to master every strategy I ever compiled. That's a lot. As of this writing, we're 90 one-hour sessions in. To warm up for one of our sessions, I gave him a challenge: "Give an impromptu speech on the state of the American economy, and after you stumble, hesitate, or falter four times, I'll cut you off. The challenge is to see how long you can go." He spoke for 20 minutes without a single mistake. After 20 minutes, he brought the impromptu speech to a perfect, persuasive, forceful, and eloquent conclusion. And he naturally and fluently used advanced strategies throughout his impromptu speech. After he closed the speech (which he did because he wanted to get on with the session), I asked him if he thought deeply about the strategies he used. He said no. He used them thoughtlessly. Why? Because he practiced them. You can too. You can practice them on your own. You don't need an audience. You don't need a coach. You don't even need to speak. Practice in your head. Practice ones that resonate with you. Practice with topics you care about.

KNOW TEN TIMES MORE THAN YOU INTEND TO SAY. And know what you do intend to say about ten times more fluently than you need to. This gives your mind room to relax, and frees up cognitive bandwidth to devote to strategy and rhetoric in real-time. Need to speak for five minutes? Be able to speak for 50. Need to read it three times to be able to deliver it smoothly? Read it 30 times.

INCORPORATE THEM IN SLIDES. You can use your slides or visual aids to help you ace complicated strategies. If you can't remember the five steps of a strategy, your slides can still follow them. Good slides aren't harder to use than bad slides.

USE THEM IN WRITTEN COMMUNICATION. You can read your speech. In some situations, this is more appropriate than impromptu or extemporaneous speaking. And if a strategy is difficult to remember in impromptu speaking, you can write it into your speech. And let's not forget about websites, emails, letters, etc.

PICK AND CHOOSE EASY ONES. Use strategies that come naturally and don't overload your mind. Those that do are counterproductive in fast-paced situations.

TAKE SMALL STEPS TO MASTERY. Practice one strategy. Practice it again. Keep going until you master it. Little by little, add to your base of strategies. But never take steps that overwhelm you. Pick a tactic. Practice it. Master it. Repeat.

MEMORIZE AN ENTIRE MESSAGE. Sometimes this is the right move. Is it a high-stakes message? Do you have the time? Do you have the energy? Given the situation, would a memorized delivery beat an impromptu, in-the-moment, spontaneous delivery? If you opt for memorizing, using advanced strategies is easy.

USE ONE AT A TIME. Pick an advanced strategy. Deliver it. Now what? Pick another advanced strategy. Deliver it. Now another. Have you been speaking for a while? Want to bring it to a close? Pick a closing strategy. For some people, using advanced strategies extemporaneously is easy, but only if they focus on one at a time.

MEMORIZE A KEY PHRASE. Deliver your impromptu message as planned, but add a few short, memorized key phrases throughout that include advanced strategies.

CREATE TALKING POINTS. Speak from a list of pre-written bullet-points; big-picture ideas you seek to convey. This is halfway between fully impromptu speaking and using a script. It's not harder to speak from a strategic and persuasively-advanced list of talking points than it is to speak from a persuasively weak list. You can either memorize your talking points, or have them in front of you as a guide.

TREAT IT LIKE A SCIENCE. At some point, you struggled with a skill that you now perform effortlessly. You mastered it. It's a habit. You do it easily, fluently, and thoughtlessly. You can do it while you daydream. Communication is the same. These tactics, methods, and strategies are not supposed to be stuck in the back of your mind as you speak. They are supposed to be ingrained in your habits.

RELY ON FLOW. In fast-paced and high-stakes situations, you usually don't plan every word, sentence, and idea consciously and deliberately. Rather, you let your subconscious mind take over. You speak from a flow state. In flow, you may flawlessly execute strategies that would have overwhelmed your conscious mind.

LISTEN TO THE PROMPTS. You read a strategy and found it difficult to use extemporaneously. But as you speak, your subconscious mind gives you a prompt:

"this strategy would work great here." Your subconscious mind saw the opportunity and surfaced the prompt. You execute it, and you do so fluently and effortlessly.

FOLLOW THE FIVE-STEP CYCLE. First, find truth. Research. Prepare. Learn. Second, define your message. Figure out what you believe about what you learned. Third, polish your message with rhetorical strategies, without distorting the precision with which it conveys the truth. Fourth, practice the polished ideas. Fifth, deliver them. The endeavor of finding truth comes before the rhetorical endeavor. First, find the right message. Then, find the best way to convey it.

CREATE YOUR OWN STRATEGY. As you learn new theories, mental models, and principles of psychology and communication, you may think of a new strategy built around the theories, models, and principles. Practice it, test it, and codify it.

STACK GOOD HABITS. An effective communicator is the product of his habits. If you want to be an effective communicator, stack good communication habits (and break bad ones). This is a gradual process. It doesn't happen overnight.

DON'T TRY TO USE THEM. Don't force it. If a strategy seems too difficult, don't try to use it. You might find yourself using it anyway when the time is right.

KNOW ONLY ONE. If you master one compelling communication strategy, like one of the many powerful three-part structures that map out a persuasive speech, that can often be enough to drastically and dramatically improve your impact.

REMEMBER THE SHORTCOMING OF MODELS. All models are wrong, but some are useful. Many of these complex strategies and theories are models. They represent reality, but they are not reality. They help you navigate the territory, but they are not the territory. They are a map, to be used if it helps you navigate, and to be discarded the moment it prevents you from navigating.

DON'T LET THEM INHIBIT YOU. Language flows from thought. You've got to have something to say. And *then* you make it as compelling as possible. And *then* you shape it into something poised and precise; persuasive and powerful; compelling and convincing. Meaning and message come first. Rhetoric comes second. Don't take all this discussion of "advanced communication strategies," "complex communication tactics," and "the deep and concrete science of communication" to suggest that the basics don't matter. They do. Tell the truth as precisely and boldly as you can. Know your subject-matter like the back of your hand. Clear your mind and focus on precisely articulating exactly what you believe to be true. Be authentic. The advanced strategies are not supposed to stand between you and your audience. They are not supposed to stand between you and your authentic and spontaneous self – they are supposed to be integrated with it. They are not an end in themselves, but a means to the end of persuading the maximum number of people to adopt truth. Trust your instinct. Trust your intuition. It won't fail you.

MASTERING ONE COMMUNICATION SKILL

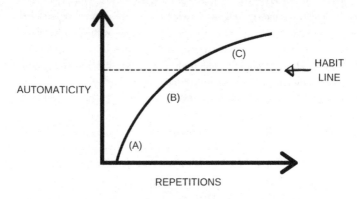

FIGURE V: Automaticity is the extent to which you do something automatically, without thinking about it. At the start of building a communication habit, it has low automaticity. You need to think about it consciously (A). After more repetitions, it gets easier and more automatic (B). Eventually, the behavior becomes more automatic than deliberate. At this point, it becomes a habit (C).

MASTERING COMMUNICATION

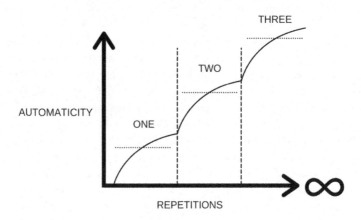

FIGURE IV: Layer good communication habits on top of each other. Go through the learning curve over and over again. When you master the first good habit, jump to the second. This pattern will take you to mastery.

THE FOUR LEVELS OF KNOWING

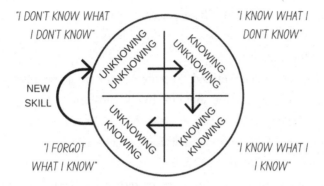

FIGURE III: First, you don't know you don't know it. Then, you discover it and know you don't know it. Then, you practice it and know you know it. Then, it becomes a habit. You forget you know it. It's ingrained in your habits.

REVISITING THE LEARNING CURVE

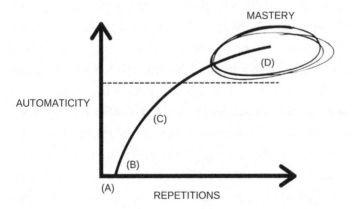

FIGURE II: Note the stages of knowing on the learning curve: unknowing unknowing (A), knowing unknowing (B), knowing knowing (C), unknowing knowing (D).

WHAT'S REALLY HAPPENING?

Have you ever thought deeply about what happens when you communicate? Let's run through the mile-high view.

At some point in your life, you bumped into an experience. You observed. You learned. The experience changed you. Your neural networks connected in new ways. New rivers of neurons began to flow through them.

The experience etched a pattern into your neurobiology representing information about the moral landscape of the universe; a map of *where we are, where we should go, and how we should make the journey.* This is meaning. This is your message.

Now, you take the floor before a crowd. Whether you realize it or not, you want to copy the neural pattern from your mind to their minds. You want to show them where we are, where we should go, and how we should make the journey.

So, you speak. You gesture. You intone. Your words convey meaning. Your body language conveys meaning. Your voice conveys meaning. You flood them with a thousand different inputs, some as subtle as the contraction of a single facial muscle, some as obvious as your opening line. Your character, your intentions, and your goals seep into your speech. Everyone can see them. Everyone can see you.

Let's step into the mind of one of your audience members. Based on all of this, based on a thousand different inputs, based on complex interactions between their conscious and nonconscious minds, the ghost in the machine steps in, and by a dint of free will, acts as the final arbiter and makes a choice. A mind is changed. You changed it. And changing it changed you. You became more confident, more articulate, and deeper; more capable, more impactful, and stronger.

Communication is connection. One mind, with a consciousness at its base, seeks to use ink or pixels or airwaves to connect to another. Through this connection, it seeks to copy neural patterns about the present, the future, and the moral landscape. Whatever your message is, the underlying connection is identical. How could it not be?

IS IT ETHICAL?

By "it," I mean deliberately using language to get someone to do or think something. Let's call this rhetoric. We could just as well call it persuasion, influence, communication, or even leadership itself.

The answer is yes. The answer is no. Rhetoric is a helping hand. It is an iron fist. It is Martin Luther King's dream. It is Stalin's nightmare. It is the "shining city on the hill." It is the iron curtain. It is "the pursuit of happiness." It is the trail of tears. It is "liberty, equality, and brotherhood." It is the reign of terror. Rhetoric is a tool. It is neither good nor evil. It is a reflection of our nature.

Rhetoric can motivate love, peace, charity, strength, patience, progress, prosperity, common sense, common purpose, courage, hope, generosity, and unity. It can also sow the seeds of division, fan the flames of tribalism, and beat back the better angels of our nature.

Rhetoric is the best of us and the worst of us. It is as good as you are. It is as evil as you are. It is as peace-loving as you are. It is as hate-mongering as you are. And I know what you are. I know my readers are generous, hardworking people who want to build a better future for themselves, for their families, and for all humankind. I know that if you have these tools in your hands, you will use them to achieve a moral mission. That's why putting them in your hands is my mission.

Joseph Chatfield said "[rhetoric] is the power to talk people out of their sober and natural opinions." I agree. But it is also the power to talk people out of their wrong and harmful opinions. And if you're using rhetoric to talk people out of their sober opinions, the problem isn't rhetoric, it's you.

In the *Institutes of Rhetoric*, Roman rhetorician Quintilian wrote the following: "The orator then, whom I am concerned to form, shall be the orator as defined by Marcus Cato, a good man, skilled in speaking. But above all he must possess the quality which Cato places first and which is in the very nature of things the greatest and most important, that is, he must be a good man. This is essential not merely on account of the fact that, if the powers of eloquence serve only to lend arms to crime, there can be nothing more pernicious than eloquence to public and private welfare alike, while I myself, who have labored to the best of my ability to contribute something of the value to oratory, shall have rendered the worst of services to mankind, if I forge these weapons not for a soldier, but for a robber."

Saint Augustine, who was trained in the classical schools of rhetoric in the 3rd century, summed it up well: "Rhetoric, after all, being the art of persuading people to accept something, whether it is true or false, would anyone dare to maintain that truth should stand there without any weapons in the hands of its defenders against falsehood; that those speakers, that is to say, who are trying to convince their hearers of what is untrue, should know how to get them on their side, to gain their attention and have them eating out of their hands by their opening remarks, while these who are defending the truth should not? That those should utter their lies briefly, clearly, plausibly, and these should state their truths in a manner too boring to listen to, too obscure to understand, and finally too repellent to believe? That those should attack the truth with specious arguments, and assert falsehoods, while these should be incapable of either defending the truth or refuting falsehood? That those, to move and force the minds of their hearers into error, should be able by their style to terrify them, move them to tears, make them laugh, give them rousing encouragement, while these on behalf of truth stumble along slow, cold and half asleep?"

THE ETHICS OF PERSUASION

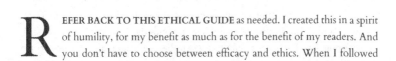

REFER BACK TO THIS ETHICAL GUIDE as needed. I created this in a spirit of humility, for my benefit as much as for the benefit of my readers. And you don't have to choose between efficacy and ethics. When I followed these principles, my words became more ethical *and* more powerful.

FOLLOW THESE TWELVE RULES. Do not use false, fabricated, misrepresented, distorted, or irrelevant evidence to support claims. Do not intentionally use specious, unsupported, or illogical reasoning. Do not represent yourself as informed or as an "expert" on a subject when you are not. Do not use irrelevant appeals to divert attention from the issue at hand. Do not cause intense but unreflective emotional reactions. Do not link your idea to emotion-laden values, motives, or goals to which it is not related. Do not hide your real purpose or self-interest, the group you represent, or your position as an advocate of a viewpoint. Do not distort, hide, or misrepresent the number, scope, or intensity of bad effects. Do not use emotional appeals that lack a basis of evidence or reasoning or that would fail if the audience examined the subject themselves. Do not oversimplify complex, gradation-laden situations into simplistic two-valued, either/or, polar views or choices. Do not pretend certainty where tentativeness and degrees of probability would be more accurate. Do not advocate something you do not believe (Johannesen et al., 2021).

APPLY THIS GOLDEN HEURISTIC. In a 500,000-word book, you might be able to tell your audience everything you know about a subject. In a five-minute persuasive speech, you can only select a small sampling of your knowledge. Would learning your entire body of knowledge result in a significantly different reaction than hearing the small sampling you selected? If the answer is yes, that's a problem.

SWING WITH THE GOOD EDGE. Rhetoric is a double-edged sword. It can express good ideas well. It can also express bad ideas well. Rhetoric makes ideas attractive; tempting; credible; persuasive. Don't use it to turn weakly-worded lies into well-worded lies. Use it to turn weakly-worded truths into well-worded truths.

TREAT TRUTH AS THE HIGHEST GOOD. Use any persuasive strategy, unless using it in your circumstances would distort the truth. The strategies should not come between you and truth, or compromise your honesty and authenticity.

AVOID THE SPIRIT OF DECEIT. Wrong statements are incorrect statements you genuinely believe. Lies are statements you know are wrong but convey anyway. Deceitful statements are not literally wrong, but you convey them with the intent to mislead, obscure, hide, or manipulate. Hiding relevant information is not literally lying (saying you conveyed all the information would be). Cherry-picking facts is not literally lying (saying there are no other facts would be). Using clever innuendo to twist reality without making any concrete claims is not literally lying (knowingly making a false accusation would be). And yet, these are all examples of deceit.

ONLY USE STRATEGIES IF THEY ARE ACCURATE. Motivate unified thinking. Inspire loving thinking. These strategies sound good. Use the victim-perpetrator-benevolence structure. Paint a common enemy. Appeal to tribal psychology. These strategies sound bad. But when reality lines up with the strategies that sound bad, they become good. They are only bad when they are inaccurate or move people down a bad path. *But the same is true for the ones that sound good.* Should Winston Churchill have motivated unified thinking? Not toward his enemy. Should he have avoided appealing to tribal psychology to strengthen the Allied war effort? Should he have avoided painting a common enemy? Should he have avoided portraying the victimization of true victims and the perpetration of a true perpetrator? Should he have avoided calling people to act as the benevolent force for good, protecting the victim and beating back the perpetrator? Don't use the victim-perpetrator-benevolence structure if there aren't clear victims and perpetrators. This is demagoguery. Painting false victims disempowers them. But if there are true victims and perpetrators, stand up for the victims and stand against the perpetrators, calling others to join you as a benevolent force for justice. Don't motivate unified thinking when standing against evil. Don't hold back from portraying a common enemy when there is one. Some strategies might sound morally suspect. Some might sound inherently good. But it depends on the situation. Every time I say "do X to achieve Y," remember the condition: "if it is accurate and moves people up a good path."

APPLY THE TARES TEST: truthfulness of message, authenticity of persuader, respect for audience, equity of persuasive appeal, and social impact (TARES).

REMEMBER THE THREE-PART VENN DIAGRAM: words that are authentic, effective, and true. Donald Miller once said "I'm the kind of person who wants to present my most honest, authentic self to the world, so I hide backstage and rehearse honest and authentic lines until the curtain opens." There's nothing dishonest or inauthentic about choosing your words carefully and making them more effective, as long as they remain just as true. Rhetoric takes a messy marble brick of truth and sculpts it into a poised, precise, and perfect statue. It takes weak truths and makes them strong. Unfortunately, it can do the same for weak lies. But preparing, strategizing, and sculpting is not inauthentic. Unskillfulness is no more authentic than skillfulness. Unpreparedness is no more authentic than preparedness.

APPLY FITZPATRICK AND GAUTHIER'S THREE-QUESTION ANALYSIS. For what purpose is persuasion being employed? Toward what choices and with what consequences for individual lives is it being used? Does the persuasion contribute to or interfere with the audience's decision-making process (Lumen, 2016)?

STRENGTHEN THE TRUTH. Rhetoric makes words strong. Use it to turn truths strong, not falsities strong. There are four categories of language: weak and wrong, strong and wrong, weak and true, strong and true. Turn weak and true language into strong and true language. Don't turn weak and wrong language into strong and wrong language, weak and true language into strong and wrong language, or strong and true language into weak and true language. Research. Question your assumptions. Strive for truth. Ensure your logic is impeccable. Defuse your biases.

START WITH FINDING TRUTH. The rhetorical endeavor starts with becoming as knowledgeable on your subject as possible and developing an impeccable logical argument. The more research you do, the more rhetoric you earn the right to use.

PUT TRUTH BEFORE STYLE. Rhetorical skill does not make you correct. Truth doesn't care about your rhetoric. If your rhetoric is brilliant, but you realize your arguments are simplistic, flawed, or biased, change course. Let logic lead style. Don't sacrifice logic to style. Don't express bad ideas well. Distinguish effective speaking from effective rational argument. Achieve both, but put reason and logic first.

AVOID THE POPULARITY VORTEX. As Plato suggested, avoid "giving the citizens what they want [in speech] with no thought to whether they will be better or worse as a result of what you are saying." Ignore the temptation to gain positive reinforcement and instant gratification from the audience with no merit to your message. Rhetoric is unethical if used solely to appeal rather than to help the world.

CONSIDER THE CONSEQUENCES. If you succeed to persuade people, will the world become better or worse? Will your audience benefit? Will you benefit? Moreover, is it the best action they could take? Or would an alternative help more? Is it an objectively worthwhile investment? Is it the best solution? Are you giving them all the facts they need to determine this on their own?

CONSIDER SECOND- AND THIRD-ORDER IMPACTS. Consider not only immediate consequences, but consequences across time. Consider the impact of the action you seek to persuade, as well as the tools you use to persuade it. Maybe the action is objectively positive, but in motivating the action, you resorted to instilling beliefs that will cause damage over time. Consider their long-term impact as well.

KNOW THAT BAD ACTORS ARE PLAYING THE SAME GAME. Bad actors already know how to be persuasive and how to spread their lies. They already know the tools. And many lies are more tempting than truth and easier to believe by their very nature. Truth waits for us to find it at the bottom of a muddy well. Truth is complicated, and complexity is harder to convey with impact. Use these tools to give truth a fighting chance in an arena where bad actors have a natural advantage. Use your knowledge to counter and defuse these tools when people misuse them.

APPLY THE FIVE ETHICAL APPROACHES: seek the greatest good for the greatest number (utilitarian); protect the rights of those affected and treat people not as means but as ends (rights); treat equals equally and nonequals fairly (justice); set the good of humanity as the basis of your moral reasoning (common good); act consistently with the ideals that lead to your self-actualization and the highest potential of your character (virtue). Say and do what is right, not what is expedient, and be willing to suffer the consequences of doing so. Don't place self-gratification, acquisitiveness, social status, and power over the common good of all humanity.

APPLY THE FOUR ETHICAL DECISION-MAKING CRITERIA: respect for individual rights to make choices, hold views, and act based on personal beliefs and values (autonomy); the maximization of benefits and the minimization of harms, acting for the benefit of others, helping others further their legitimate interests; taking action to prevent or remove possible harms (beneficence); acting in ways that cause no harm, avoid the risk of harm, and assuring benefits outweigh costs (non-maleficence); treating others according to a defensible standard (justice).

USE ILLOGICAL PROCESSES TO GET ETHICAL RESULTS. Using flawed thinking processes to get good outcomes is not unethical. Someone who disagrees should stop speaking with conviction, clarity, authority, and effective paralanguage. All are irrelevant to the truth of their words, but impact the final judgment of the audience. You must use logic and evidence to figure out the truth. But this doesn't mean logic and evidence will persuade others. Humans have two broad categories of cognitive functions: system one is intuitive, emotional, fast, heuristic-driven, and generally illogical; system two is rational, deliberate, evidence-driven, and generally logical. The best-case scenario is to get people to believe right things for right reasons (through system two). The next best case is to get people to believe right things for wrong reasons (through system one). Both are far better than letting people believe wrong things for wrong reasons. If you don't use those processes, they still function, but lead people astray. You can reverse-engineer them. If you know the truth, have an abundance of reasons to be confident you know the truth, and can predict the disasters that will occur if people don't believe the truth, don't you have a responsibility to be as effective as possible in bringing people to the truth? Logic and evidence are essential, of course. They will persuade many. They should have persuaded you. But people can't always follow a long chain of reasoning or a complicated argument. Persuade by eloquence what you learned by reason.

HELP YOUR SELF-INTEREST. (But not at the expense of your audience or without their knowledge). Ethics calls for improving the world, and you are a part of the world – the one you control most. Improving yourself is a service to others.

APPLY THE WINDOWPANE STANDARD. In Aristotle's view, rhetoric reveals how to persuade and how to defeat manipulative persuaders. Thus, top students of rhetoric would be master speakers, trained to anticipate and disarm the rhetorical tactics of their adversaries. According to this tradition, language is only useful to the extent that it does not distort reality, and good writing functions as a "windowpane," helping people peer through the wall of ignorance and view reality. You might think this precludes persuasion. You might think this calls for dry academic language. But what good is a windowpane if nobody cares to look through it? What good is a windowpane to reality if, on the other wall, a stained-glass window distorts reality but draws people to it? The best windowpane reveals as much of reality as possible while drawing as many people to it as possible.

RUN THROUGH THESE INTROSPECTIVE QUESTIONS. Are the means truly unethical or merely distasteful, unpopular, or unwise? Is the end truly good, or does it simply appear good because we desire it? Is it probable that bad means will achieve the good end? Is the same good achievable using more ethical means if we are creative, patient, and skillful? Is the good end clearly and overwhelmingly better than any bad effects of the means used to attain it? Will the use of unethical means to achieve a good end withstand public scrutiny? Could the use of unethical means be justified to those most affected and those most impartial? Can I specify my ethical criteria or standards? What is the grounding of the ethical judgment? Can I justify the reasonableness and relevancy of these standards for this case? Why are these the best criteria? Why do they take priority? How does the communication succeed or fail by these standards? What judgment is justified in this case about the degree of ethicality? Is it a narrowly focused one rather than a broad and generalized one? To whom is ethical responsibility owed – to which individuals, groups, organizations, or professions? In what ways and to what extent? Which take precedence? What is my responsibility to myself and society? How do I feel about myself after this choice? Can I continue to "live with myself?" Would I want my family to know of this choice? Does the choice reflect my ethical character? To what degree is it "out of character?" If called upon in public to justify the ethics of my communication, how adequately could I do so? What generally accepted reasons could I offer? Are there precedents which can guide me? Are there aspects of this case that set it apart from others? How thoroughly have alternatives been explored before settling on this choice? Is it less ethical than some of the workable alternatives? If the goal requires unethical communication, can I abandon the goal (Johannesen et al., 2007)?

VIEW YOURSELF AS A GUIDE. Stories have a hero, a villain who stands in his way, and a guide who helps the hero fulfill his mission. If you speak ineffectively, you are a nonfactor. If you speak deceitfully, you become the villain. But if you convey truth effectively, you become the guide in your audience's story, who leads them, teaches them, inspires them, and helps them overcome adversity and win. Use your words to put people on the best possible path. And if you hide an ugly truth, ask yourself this: "If I found out that *my* guide omitted this, how would I react?"

APPLY THE PUZZLE ANALOGY. Think of rhetoric as a piece in the puzzle of reality. Only use a rhetorical approach if it fits with the most logical, rational, and evidence-based view of reality. If it doesn't, it's the wrong puzzle piece. Try another.

KNOW THAT THE TRUTH WILL OUT. The truth can either come out in your words, or you can deceive people. You can convince them to live in a fantasy. And that might work. Until. Until truth breaks down the door and storms the building. Until the facade comes crashing down and chaos makes its entry. Slay the dragon in its lair before it comes to your village. Invite truth in through the front door before truth burns the building down. Truth wins in the end, either because a good person spreads, defends, and fights for it, or because untruth reveals itself as such by its consequences, and does so in brutal and painful fashion, hurting innocents and perpetrators alike. Trust and reputation take years to create and seconds to destroy.

MAXIMIZE THE TWO HIERARCHIES OF SUCCESS: honesty *and* effectiveness. You could say "Um, well, uh, I think that um, what we should… should uh… do, is that, well… let me think… er, I think if we are more, you know… fluid, we'll be better at… producing, I mean, progressing, and producing, and just more generally, you know, getting better results, but… I guess my point is, like, that, that if we are more fluid and do things more better, we will get better results than with a bureaucracy and, you know how it is, a silo-based structure, right? I mean… you know what I mean." Or, you could say "Bravery beats bureaucracy, courage beats the status quo, and innovation beats stagnation." Is one of those statements truer? No. Is one of them more effective? Is one of them more likely to get positive action that instantiates the truth into the world? Yes. Language is not reality. It provides signposts to reality. Two different signposts can point at the same truth – they can be equally and maximally true – and yet one can be much more effective. One gets people to follow the road. One doesn't. Maximize honesty. Then, insofar as it doesn't sacrifice honesty, maximize effectiveness. Speak truth. And speak it well.

KNOW THAT DECEPTION SINKS THE SHIP. Deception prevents perception. If someone deceives everyone onboard a ship, blinding them in a sense, they may get away with self-serving behavior. But eventually, they get hurt by the fate they designed. The ship sinks. How could it not? The waters are hazardous. If the crew is operating with distorted perceptions, they fail to see the impending dangers in the deep. So it is with teams, organizations, and entire societies.

APPLY THE WISDOM OF THIS QUOTE. Mary Beard, an American historian, author, and activist, captured the essence of ethical rhetoric well: "What politicians do is they never get the rhetoric wrong, and the price they pay is they don't speak the truth as they see it. Now, I will speak truth as I see it, and sometimes I don't get the rhetoric right. I think that's a fair trade-off." It's more than fair. It's necessary.

REMEMBER YOUR RESPONSIBILITY TO SOCIETY. Be a guardian of the truth. Speak out against wrongdoing, and do it well. The solution to evil speech is not less speech, but more (good) speech. Create order with your words, not chaos. Our civilization depends on it. Match the truth, honesty, and vulnerable transparency of your words against the irreducible complexity of the universe. And in this complex universe, remember the omnipresence of nuance, and the dangers of simplistic ideologies. (Inconveniently, simplistic ideologies are persuasive, while nuanced truths are difficult to convey. This is why good people need to be verbally skilled; to pull the extra weight of conveying a realistic worldview). Don't commit your whole mind to an isolated fragment of truth, lacking context, lacking nuance. Be precise in your speech, to ensure you are saying what you mean to say. Memorize the logical fallacies, the cognitive biases, and the rules of logic and correct thinking. (Conveniently, many rhetorical devices are also reasoning devices that focus your inquiry and help you explicate truth). But don't demonize those with good intentions and bad ideas. If they are forthcoming and honest, they are not your enemy. Rather, the two of you are on a shared mission to find the truth, partaking in a shared commitment to reason and dialogue. The malevolent enemy doesn't care about the truth. And in this complex world, remember Voltaire's warning to "cherish those who seek the truth but beware of those who find it," and Aristotle's startling observation that "the least deviation from truth [at the start] is multiplied a thousandfold." Be cautious in determining what to say with conviction. Good speaking is not a substitute for good thinking. The danger zone is being confidently incorrect. What hurts us most is what we know that just isn't so. Remember these tenets and your responsibility, and rhetoric becomes the irreplaceable aid of the good person doing good things in difficult times; the sword of the warrior of the light.

KNOW THAT DECEPTION IS ITS OWN PUNISHMENT. Knowingly uttering a falsehood is a spoken lie of commission. Having something to say but not saying it is a spoken lie of omission. Knowingly behaving inauthentically is an acted-out lie of commission. Knowingly omitting authentic behavior is an acted-out lie of omission. All these deceptions weaken your being. All these deceptions corrupt your own mind, turning your greatest asset into an ever-present companion you can no longer trust. Your conscience operates somewhat autonomously, and it will call you out (unless your repeated neglect desensitizes it). You have a conscious conscience which speaks clearly, and an unconscious conscience, which communicates more subtly. A friend of mine asked: "Why do we feel relieved when we speak truth? Why are we drawn toward it, even if it is not pleasant? Do our brains have something that makes this happen?" Yes, they do: our consciences, our inner lights, our inner north stars. And we feel relieved because living with the knowledge of our own deceit is often an unbearable burden. You live your life before an audience of one: yourself. You cannot escape the observation of your own awareness; you can't hide from yourself. Everywhere you go, there you are. Everything you do, there you are. Some of the greatest heights of wellbeing come from performing well in this one-man theater, and signaling virtue to yourself; being someone you are proud to be (and grateful to observe). Every time you lie, you tell your subconscious mind that your character is too weak to contend with the truth. And this shapes your character accordingly. It becomes true. And then what? Lying carries its own punishment, even if the only person who catches the liar is the liar himself.

BE A MONSTER (THEN LEARN TO CONTROL IT). There is nothing moral about weakness and harmlessness. The world is difficult. There are threats to confront, oppressors to resist, and tyrants to rebuff. (Peterson, 2018). There are psychopaths, sociopaths, and Machiavellian actors with no love for the common good. There is genuine malevolence. If you are incapable of being an effective deceiver, then you are incapable of being an effective advocate for truth: it is the same weapon, pointed in different directions. If you cannot use it in both directions, can you use it at all? Become a monster, become dangerous, and become capable of convincing people to believe in a lie… and then use this ability to convince them to believe in the truth. The capacity for harm is also the capacity for harming harmful entities; that is to say, defending innocent ones. If you can't hurt anyone, you can't help anyone when they need someone to stand up for them. Words are truly weapons, and the most powerful weapons in the world at that. The ability to use them, for good *or* for bad, is the prerequisite to using them for good. There is an archetype in our cultural narratives: the well-intentioned but harmless protagonist who gets roundly defeated by the villain, until he develops his monstrous edge and integrates it, at which point he becomes the triumphant hero. Along similar lines, I watched a film about an existential threat to humanity, in which the protagonist sought to convey the threat to a skeptical public, but failed miserably because he lacked the rhetorical skill to do so. The result? The world ended. Everyone died. The protagonist was of no use to anyone. And this almost became a true story. A historical study showed that in the Cuban Missile Crisis, the arguments that won out in the United States mastermind group were not the best, but those argued with the most conviction. Those with the best arguments lacked the skill to match. The world (could have) ended. The moral? Speak truth… well.

MASTERING COMMUNICATION, ONE SKILL AT A TIME

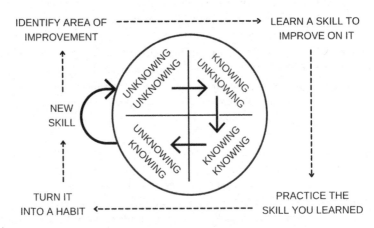

FIGURE I: The proven path to mastery.

eloquence

....

noun

   fluent or persuasive speaking or writing

eloquent

....

adjective

   clearly expressing or indicating something

CONTENTS

THE SECOND SPEECH: 135

THE THIRD SPEECH: 183

BEFORE YOU GO...

Rhetoric, Motivated by Love, Guided by Reason, and Aimed at Truth, Is a Powerful Force for the Greatest Good.

POLITICAL DISCLAIMER

Throughout this book, and throughout all my books, I draw examples of communication strategies from the political world. I quote from the speeches of many of America's great leaders, like JFK and MLK, as well as from more recent political figures of both major parties. Political communication is ideal for illustrating the concepts revealed in the books. It is the best source of examples of words that work that I have ever found. I don't use anything out of the political mainstream. And it is by extensively studying the inaugural addresses of United States Presidents and the great speeches of history that I have discovered many of the speaking strategies I share with you.

My using the words of any particular figure to illustrate a principle of communication is not necessarily an endorsement of the figure or their message. Separate the speaker from the strategy. After all, the strategy is the only reason the speaker made an appearance in the book at all. Would you rather have a weak example of a strategy you want to learn from a speaker you love, or a perfect example of the strategy from a speaker you detest?

For a time, I didn't think a disclaimer like this was necessary. I thought people would do this on their own. I thought that if people read an example of a strategy drawn from the words of a political figure they disagreed with, they would appreciate the value of the example as an instructive tool and set aside their negative feelings about the speaker. "Yes, I don't agree with this speaker or the message, but I can clearly see the strategy in this example and I now have a better understanding of how it works and how to execute it." Indeed, I suspect 95% of my readers do just that. You probably will, too. But if you are part of the 5% who aren't up for it, don't say I didn't warn you, and please don't leave a negative review because you think I endorse this person or that person. I don't, as this is strictly a book about communication.

ELOQUENCE

THE HIDDEN SECRET OF WORDS THAT CHANGE THE WORLD

SPEAK FOR SUCCESS COLLECTION BOOK

II

ELOQUENCE CHAPTER

I

THE BURIED SECRET:

Eloquence is a Millennia-Old
Science with Proven Formulas

A 2,000-YEAR-OLD PURSUIT...

W HY DO SOME WORDS WORK and change the world, while others fall flat, failing to impact, influence, and inspire anyone at all?

Why are some people graced with effortless eloquence, easily captivating complete attention at all times?

And of most importance, how can we grab this same competitive advantage for ourselves?

2,000 years ago, these same questions occupied the geniuses of antiquity: Men like Aristotle, Plato, and Socrates. And they left us answers, if we know where to look for them.

In short: There is a hidden, little-known, underground science behind words that work.

Years ago, I decided to uncover the 2,000-year-old science and the secrets of words that can change the world. And in this concise handbook of eloquence, I'll show you exactly what I found.

WHAT DOES IT MEAN FOR YOU?

What's the value of learning these proven secrets of eloquence?

It's simple: You will unlock on-demand access to the secret formulas of eloquent language presidents and world-leaders hire armies of speech-writers to produce.

Top CEOs pay thousands of dollars (or more) to an agency to produce keynotes containing these secrets. You will instantly and easily produce them with natural grace, whenever you need them.

Your message will move minds and motivate people, creating an enthusiastic and energetic response to your persuasive appeals.

You will instantly impact, influence, and inspire others, becoming a leader in the process (no matter your title).

You will quickly gain an edge in any discussion or debate.

You will speak with more confidence.

Everything you say will sound more sophisticated and important.

Nobody will ignore your proposals.

Nobody will get the wrong idea about your capabilities because your communication produces the wrong subconscious impression about who you are.

And nobody will be able to resist feeling drawn into your communication and captivated by your message.

These secrets of eloquence dominate nearly every single message that goes viral. You'll notice this once you discover them.

Every single message that moves people on a deep, emotional level uses these secrets.

Ideas standing the tests of time are enveloped in these elements of eloquence.

And the best part? You will be able to accomplish all of this by using simple, straightforward, step-by-step (though virtually secret) formulas of eloquence, acting as predictable algorithms for powerful language.

REPEATABLE ALGORITHMS AND FORMULAS

It's simple: The strategies I teach you are step-by-step strategies; fill-in formulas; plug-and-play patterns.

What do I mean by that? I will uncover an element of eloquence. I will break it down into a simple mold. You will apply the universal mold to your language, plugging your desired meaning into the "eloquence algorithm." Thus, this entire process – one formerly treated as an arcane art – becomes a simple, straightforward, predictable science, well within reach.

HOW ELOQUENCE ALGORITHMS PRODUCE INSTANT IMPACT

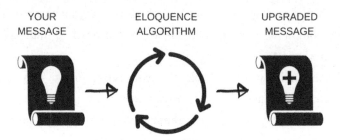

FIGURE 1: The strategies revealed in this book act as repeatable step-by-step algorithms. Provide the input parameters – your language – and run the algorithm to produce an upgraded version of the input.

Read the following three quotes...

"And so, my fellow Americans: Ask not what your country can do for you – ask what you can do for your country." – John Fitzgerald Kennedy

"My heart is a house homie; fear don't live here." – Curtis "50 Cent" Jackson

"That's 58 songs every second of every minute of every hour of every day." – Steve Jobs

What do these three items have in common?

They are all undeniably, unambiguously, unquestionably eloquent. They carry a gravitas that weaker language lacks. They compel our attention, command our intent, and resound as a clarion call from an elevated plane of being; they are all purposeful, poised, and perfect; they are all proportional, symmetrical, and attractive to the heart and mind.

Eloquence algorithms created all of them.

Prior, I felt that eloquent language was the random product of a genetically gifted writer, or a serially successful speaker; that any attempt at emulation would sound stilted. Now, I know that all eloquent language can be broken down into a simple set of algorithms; a prescription of steps that allow anybody to speak or write with the exact same surpassing eloquence, and to do so effortlessly, as easily as following a cooking recipe.

And remember: These secrets deal with rhetoric of form. What does this mean? They deal with the arrangement, proportion, and auditory appeal of language, totally separated from its meaning.

WHY DOES IT WORK?

And does it really make a difference? Yes. A big difference. Science conclusively proves it. There is a mountain of empirical evidence backed by thousands of years of anecdotal evidence supporting this conclusion. The large body of research calls it the rhyme as reason effect. I frequently refer to it as the "aesthetic impact bias."

WHAT IS THE RHYME AS REASON EFFECT?

We perceive a rhyming message as more truthful. The rhyme as reason effect evokes the aesthetic-impact bias: We judge rhetorically charged language with appealing aesthetic form as more truthful, more compelling, and more persuasive. The exact same sentiment arranged in a more aesthetically pleasing way receives drastically more support. Remember: In this context, rhyme goes far beyond words ending with the same sound, like "the *cat* in the h*at*." In this context, rhyme includes a boundless range of phonetic symmetries, like: "the party'S *St*rong, *St*eady, *St*able leader*Ship* haS kept the *Ship* of *St*ate on a *co*nSiStent *co*urSe of progreSS."

THE PSYCHOLOGY OF LINGUISTIC PERSUASION

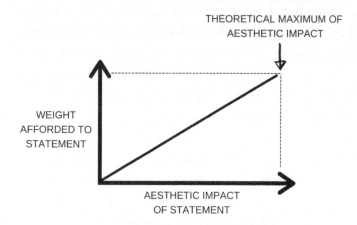

FIGURE 2: As the aesthetic impact of a statement rises, so does the weight of the statement in the minds of listeners. This is empirically and scientifically proven. The strategies in this book raise aesthetic impact.

WHAT IS AN EXAMPLE OF THE RHYME AS REASON EFFECT?

An army of speech-writers engineers every single high-stakes speech, like a presidential inaugural address, for maximum aesthetic impact. And aesthetic impact goes far beyond rhyming alone.

Quotes we remember for our entire lives, like Ben Franklin's "Early to bed and early to rise makes one healthy, wealthy and wise," exemplify this bias too. What's the proof it represents the rhyme as reason and aesthetic impact biases at work? If we reword the quote to "Early to bed and early to rise makes one healthy, wealthy, and intelligent," people systematically and predictably judge it as less truthful and valuable.

HOW DO YOU OVERCOME THE RHYME AS REASON EFFECT?

If you're comparing two messages, and only one is aesthetically pleasing, summarize both in your own language. Why? Doing so maintains their sentiment while equalizing their aesthetic appeal. Thus, the rhyme as reason effect and the aesthetic impact bias won't act on your judgement by favoring the eloquent one.

WHO DISCOVERED THE RHYME AS REASON EFFECT? WHAT DOES THE SCIENTIFIC LITERATURE SAY ABOUT IT?

In Matthew S. McGlone and Jessica Tofighbakhsh's groundbreaking paper titled *Birds of a Feather Flock Conjointly (?): Rhyme as Reason in Aphorisms*, they write the following: "We explored the role that poetic form can play in people's perceptions of the accuracy of aphorisms as descriptions of human behavior. Participants judged the ostensible accuracy of unfamiliar aphorisms presented in their textually surviving form or a semantically equivalent modified form. Extant rhyming aphorisms in their original form (e.g., "What sobriety conceals, alcohol reveals") were judged to be more accurate than modified versions that did not preserve rhyme ("What sobriety conceals, alcohol unmasks"). However, the perceived truth advantage of rhyming aphorisms over their modified forms was attenuated when people were cautioned to distinguish aphorisms' poetic qualities from their semantic content. Our results suggest that rhyme, like repetition, affords statements an enhancement in processing fluency that can be misattributed to heightened conviction about their truthfulness."

The same authors write in another paper titled *The Keats Heuristic: Rhyme as Reason in Aphorism Interpretation* the following: "Do people distinguish between the form and propositional content of a statement when evaluating its truthfulness? We asked people to judge the comprehensibility and ostensible accuracy of unfamiliar aphorisms presented in their original rhyming form (e.g., *Woes unite foes*) or a semantically equivalent non-rhyming form (*Woes unite enemies*). Although the different versions were perceived as equally comprehensible, the rhyming versions were perceived as more accurate. This 'rhyme as reason' effect suggests that in certain circumstances, people may base their judgments of a statement's truth value in part on its aesthetic qualities. Our results are consistent with models of persuasion which assume that people rely on heuristic cues to evaluate messages when they lack the evidence and/or motivation to scrutinize message content (e.g., Eagly and Chaiken, 1993)."

Petra Filkuková and Sven Hroar Klempe write in their paper titled *Rhyme as Reason in Commercial and Social Advertising* the following: "This study investigated the rhyme-as-reason effect on new artificially created advertising slogans. Rhymes and non-rhymes were in Experiment 1 and 2 compared in a between-subjects design and in Experiment 3 in a within-subjects design. The quality of the form and content of the slogans was always evaluated by separate groups. In Experiment 1, we found a strong preference for rhyming slogans as opposed to their non-rhyming counterparts. Rhymes were rated as more likeable, more original, easier to remember, more suitable for campaigns, more persuasive and more trustworthy. In Experiment 2, social advertising messages were evaluated favorably in both rhyming and non-rhyming versions. However, when participants directly compared rhymes and non-rhymes on the same scale (Experiment 3), the difference between commercial and social advertising disappeared and for all slogans rhymes were clearly preferred to non-rhymes in terms of both form and content. A detailed analysis revealed that the rhymes scoring high on formal aspects were also favored in the questionnaire investigating content aspects."

In an article published on Medium by Chris Lynch titled *"Strong and Stable" – a Lesson in the Use of Consonance, Rhyme-as-reason, and the Keats Heuristic,* he reports the following: "In experiments, subjects judged variations of sayings which did and did not rhyme, and tended to evaluate those that rhymed as more truthful (controlled for meaning). For example, the statement 'What sobriety conceals, alcohol reveals' was judged to be more accurate than by different participants who saw 'What sobriety conceals, alcohol unmasks.'"

HOW DO YOU USE THE RHYME AS REASON EFFECT IN COMMUNICATION?

This book takes a deep dive into a massive subject: Eloquence, and the secrets of rhetoric producing it. It unlocks hidden and little-known but proven and powerful rhetorical strategies discovered by legendary intellects of antiquity, stacking new discoveries on the foundation they laid 2,000 years ago. The best part? Every single one of these proven speaking patterns activates the aesthetic impact bias, rhyme as reason effect, and Keats heuristic (three names for the same bias).

In short: The secrets you learn are scientifically proven to make your words count; to get people to listen, agree, and act on what you say; to turn communication into an advantage. The evidence is empirical, and it is extensive.

THE PSYCHOLOGY OF THE ELOQUENCE ALGORITHMS

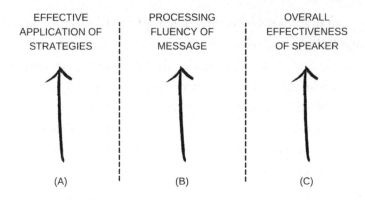

FIGURE 3: As you apply the strategies in this book, provided you do so effectively, the processing fluency of your message rises. Listeners are able to process the message – to receive, recall, analyze, judge, and otherwise interact with it – with greater ease. Processing fluency raises the persuasive impact of a message.

READ AT YOUR OWN RISK!

Just kidding.

Sort of...

Here's the thing: This book is difficult. It's short, concise, and direct; it wastes no time on needless anecdotes and pointless examples. It seeks to, in the shortest time possible, help you master the secrets of eloquence.

But the secrets can be exceedingly complex. There is no way around this, unless I am willing to simplify the subject-matter so much so that the principles themselves are lost. (And I'm not).

Extremely intelligent people struggle with some of these principles, especially the more complicated secrets.

Why? Part of the reason is that the more complicated secrets are really unique combinations of many of the simpler secrets.

It's the nature of the subject. But I've studied it for half a decade, and I want you to know this: The way the principles are presented to you here is the simplest way they can be presented without weakening them.

Why am I telling you this?

Because I want to extend a helping hand, if you need it. Confused about a secret in the book? Need more explanation or another example? Email pandreibusiness@gmail.com with the subject line "eloquence secrets help" and I'll get back to you within 12 hours.

And a brief note: I try to enumerate one secret per passage we analyze, which often means a confluence of other secrets, "sub-secrets," if you will, acting together in a unique way. But remember this: There's almost always more in the passage, so try to find it. One passage one secret is, I've found, simply the easiest way to work through the strategies for readers.

Let me be fully honest with you. This book will not entertain you. At least not on purpose. This book will not artificially extend the material to hit a preset page count. This book gets to the point. And the point is often unfamiliar and difficult. It requires close reading. If you're looking for an easy read, I recommend another book. If you're looking for an effective read – one that teaches you its subject better than any other book – then read on.

A summary of your ever-expanding rhetorical toolbox follows each chapter. These summaries provide the "building block devices" and, when possible, different permutations of these building block devices presented in the section. However, it is not exhaustive. It does not summarize every possible permutation. I trust you will find this summary a convenient method for reviewing the content should you need to.

THE RAW MATERIAL

Where did I discover these proven principles of perfect eloquence?

They are buried in the legendary words of legendary leaders. Let's begin the search.

HOW TO SPEAK LIKE HISTORY'S LEGENDARY LEADERS

FIGURE 4: This book is built around the process of analyzing a legendary speech, uncovering its strategies and tactics, packaging these strategies and tactics into a repeatable framework, collecting these frameworks in the manuscript, which you then read to learn the frameworks that you plug into your message, making it as effective as the legendary speech in which I discovered the strategy.

...............................Chapter Summary...............................

- Rhetoric is an ancient art stretching back over 2,000 years to the Ancient Greek philosophers.
- Science conclusively proves that raising the aesthetic impact of your communication raises its influence.
- This is called the rhyme as reason effect – producing "rhyme" in your language raises perception of truth.

- By reverse-engineering the legendary words of legendary leaders, we can uncover and use hidden rhetorical devices.
- These hidden rhetorical devices, used well, allow you to achieve as much eloquence as armies of speech writers.
- This book is difficult, and the material is often frustratingly complex (or so I am told). Read at your own risk.

KEY INSIGHT:

Small Linguistic Details – As Tiny As Two Words That Combine Well – Create "Rhyme."

And "Rhyme," Although It is Much More Than Mere Rhyme, Creates Eloquence and Impact.

Email Peter D. Andrei, the author of the Speak for Success collection and the President of Speak Truth Well LLC directly.

pandreibusiness@gmail.com

SPEAK FOR SUCCESS COLLECTION BOOK

II

ELOQUENCE CHAPTER

II

THE FIRST SPEECH:

Bill Clinton's First Inaugural Address

"THIS JOYFUL MOUNTAINTOP OF CELEBRATION..."

B ILL CLINTON DELIVERED THIS ADDRESS on January 20, 1993. Laced with stunning metaphors, striking figurative and visual language, and heaps of religious imagery, Clinton's first inaugural address provides an undeniable call to service, selflessness, and self-transcendence. He taps into the lifeward instinct: the desire to transcend and transform; to be reborn anew; to rise, growing better, stronger, more virtuous, and more fully actualized – globally, nationally, communally, and individually. Let us begin.

PASSAGE #1:

My fellow citizens: Today we celebrate the mystery of American renewal. This ceremony is held in the depth of winter. But, by the words we speak and the faces we show the world, we force the spring. A spring reborn in the world's oldest democracy, that brings forth the vision and courage to reinvent America.

SECRET #1:

The power of "we."

"We" is a magic word. It carries inherent psychological appeal. And it is deeply eloquent, captivating people and drawing them into your message. Why? It puts people on a plane of amicability with the speaker (or writer – henceforth, "speaker" refers to both), fostering a connection through which meaning easily flows. In using "we," Clinton becomes the spokesperson for a psychological coalition.

We are biased to judge the members of our psychological coalition more favorably than they merit. This is a cognitive bias: a repetitive, predictable thinking process you can activate to influence human judgement. Rhetorical strategies almost always activate cognitive biases in a positive way, using bad thinking to promote positive ends.

THE SECRET OF INCLUSIVE LANGUAGE

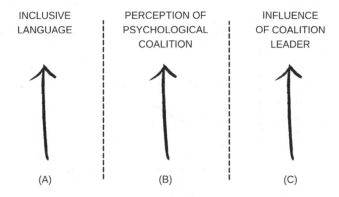

FIGURE 5: Inclusive language produces a psychological coalition. A psychological coalition is a "tribe" of people united in common cause. The leader of the coalition has massive influence over the members of the coalition.

THE POWER OF PSYCHOLOGICAL COALITIONS

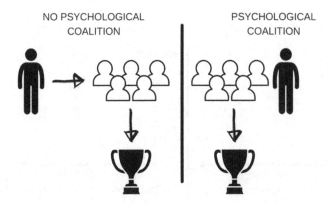

FIGURE 6: A psychological coalition turns a boss into a leader. In the absence of a psychological coalition, your calls to action sound like "Hey! You! Go do this, or else!" With the coalition, they sound like "Let's go do this together, so we may all benefit."

HOW RHETORICAL STRATEGIES ACTIVATE "BIASES"

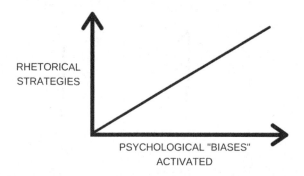

FIGURE 7: A cognitive bias is a repetitive and faulty thinking process. For example, people have an availability bias: the more easily they can recall information, the more they value it and the more it influences them. Rhetorical strategies activate cognitive biases in your favor.

THE LITTLE-KNOWN "LOLLAPALOOZA EFFECT"

STRATEGY STACKING CREATES THE LOLLAPALOOZA EFFECT

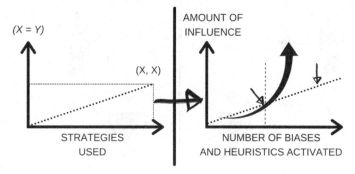

FIGURE 8: Activating multiple biases in the same direction at once creates a massive non-linear increase in influence.

PASSAGE #2:

When our founders boldly declared America's independence to the world and our purposes to the Almighty, they knew that America, to endure, would have to change. Not change for change's sake, but change to preserve America's ideals; life, liberty, the pursuit of happiness. Though we march to the music of our time, our mission is timeless. Each generation of Americans must define what it means to be an American.

SECRET #2:

Double thematic repetition: lens and subject.

Your subject is what you're talking about. Your theme is the lens through which you photograph that subject. It can alter its appearance, emphasizing or deemphasizing aspects of it, even making it seem like an entirely different thing altogether. You should be able to summarize your theme and subject in a single word each. For Clinton? His subject is America. His theme is change.

THE RIGHT THEME PRODUCES PERSUASIVE POWER

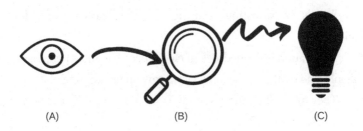

(A)　　　　　　　(B)　　　　　　　(C)

FIGURE 9: Your theme – or lens (B) – shapes human perception (A) of your subject (C).

And in this passage, we can see that he repeats "America" and "change" over and over and over. Why? Because repetition is inherently eloquent, electrifying the audience. But more importantly, because by repeating his subject and his "lens" in such close proximity and with such frequency, he solidifies a neural association – or connection – between "America" and "change."

It's simple: Neural associations are formed between items occurring together frequently. He presents the two items together frequently, and so "America" becomes neurologically connected to "change." Henceforth, thinking "America" triggers "change," and vice-versa.

PASSAGE #3:

On behalf of our nation, I salute my predecessor, President Bush, for his half-century of service to America. And I thank the millions of men and women whose steadfastness and sacrifice triumphed over Depression, fascism and Communism.

SECRET #3:

Fragmented alliterative couplet (and reverse alliterative tricolon).

Words in proximity starting with the same sound form alliteration.

Alliteration is the bedrock of eloquence. And most people, even people who do this for a living, lack a true understanding of it.

They think alliteration is simply something like this, and nothing more: "*S*trong *s*tate."

They're wrong. Well, they're not *wrong* – they're just not completely right. Why? Because alliteration is significantly more malleable and flexible a rhetorical device than two words smacked right up against each other starting with the same sound.

For example, Clinton uses a fragmented alliterative couplet in this passage: "*S*teadfastness and *s*acrifice." The conjunction "and" fragments it.

And he uses reverse alliteration (otherwise known as "rhyming") in a tricolon (a comma-delineated list of three; another compelling and eloquent strategy): "Depression, fasci*sm*, and commun*ism*."

PASSAGE #4:

Today, a generation raised in the shadows of the Cold War assumes new responsibilities in a world warmed by the sunshine of freedom but threatened still by ancient hatreds and new plagues.

SECRET #4:

Nested contrasts and symmetries.

Contrast is an essential element of eloquence, as foundational as alliteration.

Human understanding of meaning grows deeper yet more fluent if compelling contrasts envelop the meaning. Why? Because our perception itself is defined by comparison between inputs.

Clinton contrasts shadows with sunshine, the Cold War with a world warmed, warmed with threatened, new responsibilities with ancient hatreds and new plagues, and ancient hatreds with new plagues. And possibly even more I missed.

There's a sort of meta-contrast going on here too: A contrast between contrasts and symmetries. Because while the passage is rife with contrasts, there are also symmetries, most notably in the structure of the sentences.

For example: "...in the shadows of the Cold War" and "...in the sunshine of freedom."

This represents contrasting ideas nested in symmetric sentences, forming compelling meta-contrast.

PASSAGE #5:

Raised in unrivaled prosperity, we inherit an economy that is still the world's strongest, but is weakened by business failures, stagnant wages, increasing inequality, and deep divisions among our people.

SECRET #5:

Intensifying superabundance.

What is superabundance? The expansion of an idea into a mountain of flowing, water-falling, fluent language; often language identifying different aspects of the idea, with the idea broken down into its constituent parts.

Clinton's essential message is this: "The United States has a struggling economy."

The superabundance attached to this message is this: "weakened by business failures, stagnant wages, increasing inequality, and deep divisions among our people."

Which is more compelling? Which is more eloquent? The message itself? Or the message and the following superabundance which vindicates it with a mountain of intense, short, snappy examples? The answer is self-evident.

PASSAGE #6:

When George Washington first took the oath I have just sworn to uphold, news traveled slowly across the land by horseback and across the ocean by boat. Now, the sights and sounds of this ceremony are broadcast instantaneously to billions around the world.

SECRET #6:

Specific, action-oriented "verb-saturated" language.

Verbs work. They captivate. They draw people in. They produce easy eloquence and simplify your message. Why? Because they present information how the human mind is wired to receive it: In terms of actions; in terms of "item one" doing "action" to "item two."

This passage is filled with language saturated by verbs, creating a sort of specific, action-oriented narrative, seemingly driven forward by its own momentum.

It is eloquent and captivating because the human mind cannot help seeing the actions taking place: "When George Washington first took the oath I have just sworn to uphold (irresistible mental movie of George Washington taking oath), news traveled slowly across the land by horseback (irresistible mental movie of news travelling slowly across land by horseback) and across the ocean by boat (irresistible mental movie of news traveling across the ocean by boat). Now, the sights and sounds of this ceremony are broadcast instantaneously to billions around the world (irresistible mental movie of sights and sounds being broadcast to millions around the world)."

PASSAGE #7:

Communications and commerce are global; investment is mobile; technology is almost magical; and ambition for a better life is now universal. We earn our livelihood in peaceful competition with people all across the earth.

SECRET #7:

Layered devices with in-flow and out-flow: alliterative couplets, fragmented alliterative couplets, reverse fragmented alliteration, "enumeratio," assonance, consonance loose parallelism, front-back alliteration, and more...

I told you it would get complicated...

Let's first define all the terms we're working with here.

Layered devices are what they sound like: Different rhetorical devices layered over each other.

In-flow and out-flow refers to different devices flowing in and out of each other, particularly when a single word or phrase or sentence or unit of meaning marks the end of the previous one and the start of the next one, as if they flow in and out of each other, overlapping only on that unit of meaning (whether it's a word, sentence, or something bigger).

Fragmented alliterative couplets, you already know: Two words relatively close to each other starting with the same sound, with an intervening word or phrase. This is the first of the devices layered over each other and flowing in and out of each other in this passage.

Alliterative couplets lack the intervening word(s).

Reverse alliteration, you already know too; and you know fragmented alliteration as well. So, putting those together, you get a clear picture of reverse fragmented alliteration: Words that "rhyme" in the traditional sense of the word separated by an intervening word or phrase.

Enumeratio is a form of superabundance: Latin for "enumeration" or "to enumerate," enumeratio produces a superabundance that is – you guessed it – an enumeration of a previous idea, statement, or concept.

Assonance is the close repetition of a vowel sound in a sentence. Recall this quote from Curtis "50 Cent" Jackson (a rapper who, believe it or not, uses the same devices as Clinton and Ronald Reagan): "My heart is a house homie; fear don't live here." See the assonance giving it a sort of flowy, eloquent appeal?

Consonance is the close repetition of a consonant sound in a sentence.

Parallelism describes sentences with mirrored grammatical structure. There are a few kinds of parallelism, which, of course, we'll shortly discuss. Loose parallelism describes sentences with roughly the same grammatical structure, minus a few exceptions.

Front-back alliteration is when the start of one word alliterates with the end of a subsequent word.

And that's about it. We're only talking about this phrase: "Communications and commerce are global; investment is mobile; technology is almost magical; and ambition for a better life is now universal." There's more in the following sentence, but we won't get into that.

So: Let's break down the quote.

Fragmented alliterative couplet: "*comm*unication and *comm*erce."

Alliterative couplets: "*a*nd *a*mbition." And "*i*nvestment *i*s."

Reverse fragmented alliteration: "Communications and commerce are glob*al*; investment is mob*ile (similar sound to 'al')*; technology is almost magic*al*; and ambition for a better life is now univers*al*."

Enumeratio: The whole passage is enumerating elements of one of Clinton's core themes, specifically change.

Assonance: "C*o*mmunicati*o*ns and c*o*mmerce are gl*o*bal; investment is m*o*bile; techn*o*l*o*gy is alm*o*st magical; and ambiti*o*n f*o*r a better life is n*ow* universal."

Consonance: "Co*mm*unications and co*mm*erce are global; invest*m*ent is *m*obile; technology is al*m*ost *m*agical; and a*m*bition for a better life is now universal."

Loose parallelism: "Communications and commerce are global (X is Y); investment is mobile (X is Y); technology is almost magical (X is Y); and ambition for a better life is now universal (X is Y)."

Front-back alliteration: "*a*lmost magic*al*."

KEY INSIGHT:

Alliteration, in All its Forms, Creates an Eloquent Drum-Beat of Symmetry, Fluency, and Flow.

Words Starting with the Same Letter Are "Synapticly Close." One Often Implies the Other.

PASSAGE #8:

Profound and powerful forces are shaking and remaking our world, and the urgent question of our time is whether we can make change our friend and not our enemy.

SECRET #8:

Stacked phonetically-undone couplets.

A "phonetically-undone couplet" is a complicated but extremely eloquent and uniquely captivating technique. The "phonetics" of a word are its *sounds*. The dominant phonetic characteristics of a word are the most noticeable and defining ones, which almost seem to announce themselves, and which dominate the sound of the word. A "phonetically undone couplet" is two words in close proximity (with usually no more than one word in between, and then only a short conjunction), which have dominant phonetic characteristics that reverse, or *almost* reverse each other's order.

For example: "Profound and powerful" seem to undo each other. The reason? Their dominant phonetic characteristics, or at least some of them, mirror each other. The dominant phonetic characteristics defining the first half of the word "profound" define the second half of the word "powerful" and the dominant phonetic characteristics defining the first half of the word "powerful" define the second half of the word "profound." Of course, this is a rough symmetry. I could enumerate these characteristics, but there's no need: the mirroring announces itself already. Another example is "shaking and remaking."

PASSAGE #9:

This new world has already enriched the lives of millions of Americans who are able to compete and win in it. But when most people are working harder for less; when others cannot work at all; when the cost of health care devastates families and threatens to bankrupt many of our enterprises, great and small; when fear of crime robs law-abiding citizens of their freedom; and when millions of poor children cannot even imagine the lives we are calling them to lead, we have not made change our friend.

SECRET #9:

"X does Y to Z:" a self-driven rhetorical narrative.

We see a continuation of action-oriented, verb-saturated language. It is extremely eloquent because "item one acts on item two" is more intuitive to the human mind than "item one is adjective."

By using this kind of language, Clinton creates a compelling rhetorical narrative. And humans think in narratives.

THE COMPLEX PSYCHOLOGY OF COMPELLING NARRATIVES

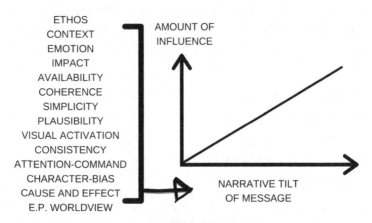

FIGURE 10: Stories are inherently persuasive structures for passing on information. They activate countless biases and heuristics. While the full discussion of the psychology of narratives is beyond the scope of this book, know that as the narrative tilt of your message rises, the amount of influence it carries rises as well. Further, as stories encompass so many biases and heuristics, they can singlehandedly trigger Lollapalooza effects.

PASSAGE #10:

We know we have to face hard truths and take strong steps. But we have not done so. Instead, we have drifted, and that drifting has eroded our resources, fractured our economy, and shaken our confidence.

SECRET #10:

Strict-parallel tricolon.

You already know tricolons: Comma-delineated lists of three.

And you know parallelism.

But what about strict parallelism?

Strict parallelism refers to parallel segments with *precisely* mirrored grammatical structures: "...eroded our resources, fractured our economy, and shaken our confidence."

(verb)ed our (noun), (verb)ed our (noun), and (verb)ed our (noun).

The symmetry in the structure mirrors the symmetry in the meaning of the words, creating compelling and eloquent coherence between the meaning of the words and their presentation. And the effect is intensified with the repetition of "our," which itself is an inclusive word with a similar effect as "we."

PASSAGE #11:

Though our challenges are fearsome, so are our strengths. And Americans have ever been a restless, questing, hopeful people. We must bring to our task today the vision and will of those who came before us. From our revolution, the Civil War, to the Great Depression to the civil rights movement, our people have always mustered the determination to construct from these crises the pillars of our history.

SECRET #11:

Asyndeton: omitted conjunctions.

Asyndeton is the omission of grammatically necessary conjunctions, raising pace, creating rhythm, and heightening intensity.

"...restless, questing, hopeful people" should, in theory, be "restless, questing, *and* hopeful people." But which is more captivating? Which creates a more compelling rhythm? Which is more intense and eloquent? In this case, asyndeton wins out.

PASSAGE #12:

Thomas Jefferson believed that to preserve the very foundations of our nation, we would need dramatic change from time to time. Well, my fellow citizens, this is our time. Let us embrace it.

SECRET #12:

X, Z, YX micro-pattern-interrupts.

A pattern interrupt is the sudden breaking away from an established pattern of communication. Pattern interrupts captivate attention. Why? Humans are pattern-recognizing creatures. We recognize a new stimulus, we observe it until we perceive its predominating patterns, we observe these patterns, and then we let them fade into the background as they grow predictable. Why? Our minds are designed to direct attention to potentially dangerous stimuli (which predictable things tend not to be).

HOW TO AVOID ACCIDENTALLY BORING YOUR AUDIENCE

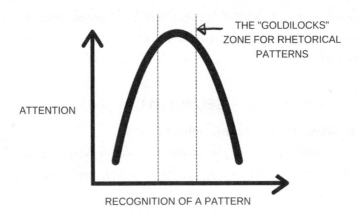

FIGURE 11: As your audience begins to perceive your pattern (or as your pattern begins to announce itself to their perception), attention rises. The pattern continues to captivate attention until it reaches the point of habituation. At this point – which can come quickly – the pattern

becomes rote, routine, boring, and droning. As they see the pattern continuing, their attention dips. Bring your patterns to the goldilocks zone, but no further. Unfortunately, there is no hard and fast rule for determining the point of habituation. It depends on the nature of the pattern in question.

So: A technique which achieves easy eloquence and controls attention is establishing a pattern until people recognize it to the point of forming expectations of what comes next, and then shattering those expectations.

Now: What's a micro-pattern-interrupt? Whenever you see a technique preceded by the word micro, it simply means the technique is occurring at the level of individual words, syllables, or even letters, not at the higher level of phrases, sentences, and larger segments of meaning.

WHY PATTERN-INTERRUPTS HOOK AUDIENCE ATTENTION

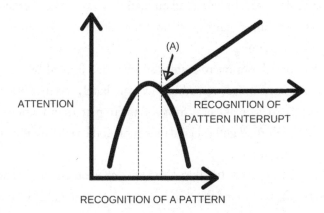

FIGURE 12: Up to the point of habituation, patterns grab attention. After the point of habituation, patterns lose attention. After the point of habituation, pattern-interrupts grab attention. The ideal sequence is this: produce rhetorical patterns until the point of habituation. Then,

> apply a pattern-interrupt. This guarantees attention rises
> (or at least doesn't fall) throughout.

This is how you use the establishment of patterns and pattern interrupts to control attention.

And while micro-pattern-interrupts miss out on the benefits of regular pattern-interrupts I mentioned just now, they gain the immense benefit of word-level eloquence: Eloquence that seems to be baked into the very fabric of your communication, the product of tiny details creating a compelling big picture.

Micro-pattern interrupts are so small and subtle they sneak under the radar. People don't observe the pattern. Instead, they subconsciously see the scheme only when you've completed the pattern-interrupt, which subtly clues them into the micro-pattern you built, sneaking under their awareness but creating appealing eloquence nonetheless (or perhaps, as a result).

Check out this segment: "Thomas Jefferson believed that to preserve the very foundations of our nation we would need dramatic change from time to time. Well, my fellow citizens, this is our time."

Eloquent, right?

It establishes a micro-pattern so small it's formed by a single word repeated twice; something we can barely even consider a pattern. Then, it breaks away from this micro-pattern in a subtle way, including a third, slightly altered repetition of the word, illuminating the previous pattern.

It's "X, X, YX." It's this: "Thomas Jefferson believed that to preserve the very foundations of our nation we would need dramatic change from time (X) to time (X). Well, my fellow citizens, this is our (Y) time (X)."

Time (X), time (X), our (Y) time (X).

PASSAGE #13:

Our democracy must be not only the envy of the world but the engine of our own renewal. There is nothing wrong with America that cannot be cured by what is right with America.

SECRET #13:

Simple contrast.

This passage portrays simple contrasts. Clinton contrasts what is "right with America" with what is "wrong with America." And this simple contrast creates compelling eloquence: Even just one set of opposites rouses the human mind by being overperceived (as human perception functions in large part through contrast), creating eloquence and grabbing attention.

HOW THE CONTRAST EFFECT SHAPES PERCEPTION

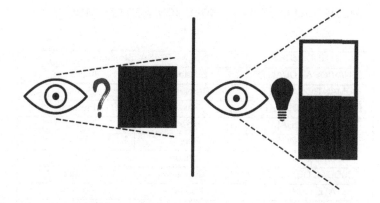

FIGURE 13: Human perception functions through contrasts. We judge items by drawing comparisons between the item in questions and other available items: contextual items, items in memory, or items provided by the speaker. Provide contrasting items which improve the estimation of the item in question. Make your idea appear

better both by raising its appeal directly and contrasting it with weaker ideas.

THE CONTRAST EFFECT AND THE "PASA" STRUCTURE

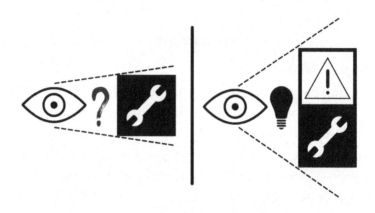

FIGURE 14: The Problem / Solution structure contrasts solutions with problems, strengthening the solution.

THE PROBLEM, AGITATE, SOLUTION, AGITATE STRUCTURE

STRUCTURE	"PASA" Structure			
BEHAVIORAL DUALITY	Escape		Approach	
SEMANTIC DUALITY	Problem		Solution	
EMOTIONAL DUALITY	Pain		Pleasure	
TEMPORAL DUALITY	Now		Later	
EXISTENTIAL DUALITY	Here		There	
DESIRE DUALITY	Aversion		Desire	
MODAL DUALITY	Chaos		Order	
STATE DUALITY	Actual		Potential	
THE SEQUENCE	**Problem**	**Agitate**	**Solution**	**Agitate**

USING CONTRAST TO IMPROVE YOUR MESSAGE

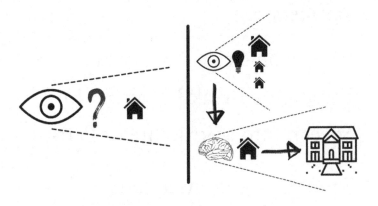

FIGURE 15: We can split the set of concepts available to your audience when they are judging your concept into two subsets: the set of target items (the concepts you seek to advance) and the set of contextual items (all other relevant and available concepts). The art of using the contrast effect is shaping the set of contextual items to contrast more positively with the target item. $100 seems great next to $1. $100 seems meaningless next to $100,000,000. For example, real estate agents artificially add subpar homes to the set of contextual items, which massively raises the perception of the target item: the home they seek to sell.

PASSAGE #14:

And so today, we pledge an end to the era of deadlock and drift; a new season of American renewal has begun. To renew America, we must be bold. We must do what no generation has had to do before. We must invest more in our own people, in their jobs, in their future, and at the same time cut our massive debt. And we must do so in a world in which we must compete for every opportunity. It will not be easy; it will require sacrifice. But it can be done, and done fairly, not choosing sacrifice for its own sake, but for our own sake. We must provide for our nation the way a family provides for its children.

KEY INSIGHT:

Paragraph-Scale Anaphora Paradigms Break Up an Entire Speech into a Structure of Parts.

Sentence-Scale Anaphora Sequences Build Rhythm and Unite a Set of Sentences.

SECRET #14:

Fragmented anaphora paradigm layered over two stacked X, YX pattern-interrupts.

So: What's anaphora? It's starting a series of segments with the same words. It builds a compelling rhythm, produces natural repetition, and sounds appealing and dramatically eloquent.

What about fragmented anaphora? Fragmented anaphora starts a series of *non-subsequent* segments with the same words: "And so today, we pledge an end to the era of deadlock and drift; a new season of American renewal has begun. To renew America, *we must* be bold. *We must* do what no generation has had to do before. *We must* invest more in our own people, in their jobs, in their future, and at the same time cut our massive debt. *And we must* do so in a world in which we must compete for every opportunity. It will not be easy; it will require sacrifice. But it can be done, and done fairly, not choosing sacrifice for its own sake, but for our own sake. *We must* provide for our nation the way a family provides for its children."

And what are X, YX pattern-interrupts?

Well: You know pattern-interrupts. You know X, X, YX pattern-interrupts. This is just a new form of pattern-interrupts. And it's a micro pattern-interrupt in this instance. You're beginning to capture all of this material. In fact, I bet you already know how X, YX pattern interrupts work: just subtract an X from the micro-pattern-interrupt we just covered. (X, X, YX) minus (X). First X, which alone is not a pattern (obviously), then YX: A slightly modified version of X, hinting at a pattern and getting our perceptional machinery engaged. Clinton stacks two of these pattern interrupts. He forms a pattern out of four phrases: the first two form a micro-pattern interrupt, as do the second two. He forms a pattern and a symmetry out of clumps of phrases that themselves form and break patterns.

"But it can be done (X), and done fairly (YX), not choosing sacrifice for its own sake (X), but for our own sake (YX)."

PASSAGE #15:

Our Founders saw themselves in the light of posterity. We can do no less. Anyone who has ever watched a child's eyes wander into sleep knows what posterity is. Posterity is the world to come; the world for whom we hold our ideals, from whom we have borrowed our planet, and to whom we bear sacred responsibility. We must do what America does best: offer more opportunity to all and demand responsibility from all.

SECRET #15:

A, B1X, C1Y, D1Z construction.

We're getting into more complicated territory here. This is a fascinating part of studying eloquence: Breaking powerful sentences down into their basic structure, and filling the structure with your words. The X, X, YX and X, YX pattern interrupts were just a brief preview of this tactic.

HOW TO FORMULIZE LEGENDARY LANGUAGE FOR EASY USE

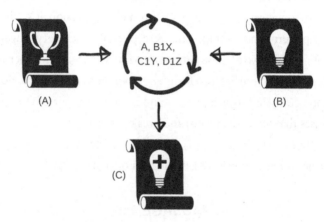

FIGURE 16: Extrapolating these sentence formulas is just another eloquence algorithm. It is the art of identifying powerful sentence structures in legendary speeches (A), generalizing and abstracting those structures into formulas, and plugging your message into it (B), which yields an improved version (C).

What's an "A, B1X, C1Y, D1Z" construction? If you've ever taken an Algebra class, you are familiar with the concept of variables acting as placeholders for unknowns. Well: Those letters and numbers are just placeholders, in a sense.

"Posterity is the world to come; the world (A) *for* (B) whom (1) we hold our ideals (X), *from* (C) whom (1) we have borrowed our planet (Y), and *to* (D) whom (1) we bear sacred responsibility (Z)."

The only constancy is the repetition of "1," a variable acting as a placeholder for, in this case, the word "whom." This defines the construction. B, C, and D stand for "for, from, and to" respectively. A stands for the introduction to the paradigm. X, Y, and Z stand as expansions of what B1, C1, and D1 outlined.

This is complicated, so I'll create an example of how you could use this structure. A: "My goal is to save this company, a company..." B1X: "under (B) which (1) we have all dedicated years of faithful and loyal service (X)..." C1Y: "to (C) which (1) we owe our gratitude for its generosity (Y)..." D1Z: "and upon (D) which (1) tens of thousands of customers rely (Z)."

PASSAGE #16:

It is time to break the bad habit of expecting something for nothing, from our government or from each other. Let us all take more responsibility, not only for ourselves and our families but for our communities and our country. To renew America, we must revitalize our democracy.

SECRET #16:

Stacked micro-parallel constructions.

Remember the difference between layered rhetorical constructions and constructions with in-flow and out-flow: Layered constructions overlap more than they stand alone, while constructions with in-flow and out-flow stand alone more than they overlap. What about stacked constructions? Stacked constructions push right up against each other, but don't overlap at all, not even on a single word.

In summary, layered rhetorical devices mostly overlap, in- and out-flowing rhetorical devices mostly don't overlap but do overlap to a lesser degree, and stacked rhetorical devices don't overlap at all, but leave no in-between space.

Eloquent language seems to possess a particular balance; a sort of arrangement in which each phrase isn't too heavy or too light, but flows appropriately and proportionately with the rest.

And in addition to this balance, eloquent language possesses innate symmetries: Structural symmetries (parallelism), but also symmetrical word choice.

This passage presents both: "It is time to break the bad habit of expecting *something for nothing*, *from our* government (phrase one, parallel to phrase two) or *from* each other (phrase two). Let us all take more responsibility, not only *for our*selves and *our* families (phrase one, parallel to phrase two) but *for our* communities and *our* country (phrase two).

Micro-parallelism creates the sense of inner balance and proportionality, which is eloquent and appealing. And word repetition, especially when stacked on top of micro-parallelism, produces the sense of symmetry. The italics indicate the symmetrical word choice.

PASSAGE #17:

This beautiful capital, like every capital since the dawn of civilization, is often a place of intrigue and calculation. Powerful people maneuver for position and worry endlessly about who is in and who is out, who is up and who is down, forgetting those people whose toil and sweat sends us here and pays our way.

SECRET #17:

Noun couplets and stacked contrasts within stacked micro-parallel constructions containing symmetrical word choice: parallelism within parallelism.

What's a noun couplet? Noun couplets are exactly what they sound like: Nouns in pairs. They are particularly evocative, connoting a uniquely critical sentiment in a precise way, such that no other words could seem to take their place.

And we talked about balance and symmetry. Noun couplets achieve both. Noun couplets are about as micro as parallel structures get: "(noun) and (noun)."

"This beautiful capital, like every capital since the dawn of civilization, is often a place of *intrigue and calculation.* Powerful people maneuver for position and worry endlessly about who is in and who is out, who is up and who is down, forgetting those people whose *toil and sweat* sends us here and pays our way."

Doesn't that sound more compelling than "...is often a place of intrigue?" Or "whose toil sends us here?" Doesn't it sound more complete and captivating?

But I want to focus on this segment: "who is in and who is out, who is up and who is down."

It's parallelism: "who is in (micro-parallel phrase one) and who is out (phrase two)."

It's stacked parallelism, because "who is up (micro-parallel phrase one) and who is out (phrase two)" follows immediately after.

And this forms a sequence of four parallel phrases: "who is in (1) and who is out (2), who is up (3) and who is down (4)."

PASSAGE #18:

Americans deserve better, and in this city today, there are people who want to do better. And so I say to all of us here, let us resolve to reform our politics, so that power and privilege no longer shout down the voice of the people. Let us put aside personal advantage so that we can feel the pain and see the promise of America. Let us resolve to make our government a place for what Franklin Roosevelt called "bold, persistent experimentation," a government for our tomorrows, not our yesterdays. Let us give this capital back to the people to whom it belongs.

SECRET #18:

Long-form fragmented alliteration.

Long-form fragmented alliteration – alliteration fragmented by significant intervening words – can provide a subtle but compelling jolt: It is extremely eloquent, and can unite an entire passage, sentence, or paragraph by creating common aesthetic appeal.

"And so I say to all of us here, let us resolve to reform our *p*olitics, so that *p*ower and *p*rivilege no longer shout down the voice of the *p*eople. Let us *p*ut aside *p*ersonal advantage so that we can feel the *p*ain and see the *p*romise of America." It flows. And it's poetic. It works. It captivates and compels. It controls attention.

PASSAGE #19:

To renew America, we must meet challenges abroad as well at home. There is no longer division between what is foreign and what is domestic; the world economy, the world environment, the world AIDS crisis, the world arms race; they affect us all.

SECRET #19:

Strict micro-repetition.

Strict micro-repetition is what most of us think of, intuitively, as repetition: Repeating a word. Are there other types of repetition? Many. And we'll get into them later on.

But why does strict micro-repetition work? Because it's not repeating a word in an unnatural way, but weaving the repetition into a compelling sequence of words serving a purpose beyond repetition.

Now: Repetition is incredibly powerful simply due to how it sounds and the effect the rhythm has on the audience. But strict micro-repetition, how Clinton used it, also serves to cement a concept, position, or idea.

"There is no longer division between what is foreign and what is domestic; the *world* economy, the *world* environment, the *world* AIDS crisis, the *world* arms race; they affect us all."

The repetition of the word "world," aside from its aesthetic appeal, cements the initial point: "There is no longer division between what is foreign and what is domestic" Further, there is an "illusory truth effect." Countless scientific studies empirically prove that people perceive statements they have heard multiple times as more truthful. Repetition creates the perception of truth.

PASSAGE #20:

Today, as an old order passes, the new world is more free but less stable. Communism's collapse has called forth old animosities and new dangers. Clearly America must continue to lead the world we did so much to make.

SECRET #20:

Repeated contrasts.

This passage should have reminded you of a previous one: "Today, a generation raised in the shadows of the Cold War assumes new responsibilities in a world warmed by the sunshine of freedom but threatened still by ancient hatreds and new plagues."

Why? Because they both carry compelling and repeated contrasts, calling on similar subject matter.

"Old order" contrasts with "new world."

"More" contrasts with "less," and "free" with "stable."

"Old animosities" contrasts with "new dangers," repeating the contrast of "old" and "new," cementing the theme of change we discussed previously.

And a brief point: There's a specific kind of contrast known as floating opposites, following this format: "Adjective A Noun A, Adjective B Noun B," where adjective A contrasts with adjective B and noun A contrasts with noun B.

"Old animosities and new dangers" is not an example of floating opposites: Adjective A ("old") contrasts with adjective B ("new"), but "animosities" (noun A) and "dangers" (noun B) don't contrast.

This is the real example of floating opposites: "Today, as an old order passes, the new world is *more* (adjective A) *free* (adjective A1) but *less* (adjective B) *stable* (adjective B1)."

But wait: Weren't they supposed to be nouns? Not necessarily. Floating opposites work just the same in the manner Clinton used them. But I presented it that way, as two nouns and two adjectives, because, as I'm sure you'll find, floating opposites tend to naturally flow into that format as you try to create them.

PASSAGE #21:

While America rebuilds at home, we will not shrink from the challenges, nor fail to seize the opportunities, of this new world. Together with our friends and allies, we will work to shape change, lest it engulf us.

SECRET #21:

"While" constructions.

"While" constructions easily sneak context for what you're about to say into your communication.

Furthermore, they act as a transition. And transitions are a prerequisite for eloquence. Why? Because they guarantee you don't lose attention when moving from one idea to the next. They act as a bridge between meaningful words and sequences, carrying people from one substantive statement to the next one.

Without transitions, people get confused. And confused minds stop listening. Transitions guarantee coherence. "While" constructions transition to another idea by illuminating what else is occurring concurrently. Used creatively, these carry the potential for tremendous eloquence. Clinton used this strategy to transition from domestic affairs to international affairs.

PASSAGE #22:

When our vital interests are challenged, or the will and conscience of the international community is defied, we will act; with peaceful diplomacy whenever possible, with force when necessary. The brave Americans serving our nation today in the Persian Gulf, in Somalia, and wherever else they stand are testament to our resolve.

SECRET #22:

Attached adjectives.

Technically all adjectives are "attached," by definition. But the term attached adjectives specifically refers to adjectives directly next to the word they modify.

Attached adjectives are a staple of eloquence. They are deeply compelling. "When our *vital* interests are challenged, or the will and conscience of the international community is defied, we will act; with *peaceful* diplomacy whenever possible, with force when necessary. The *brave* Americans serving our nation today in the Persian Gulf, in Somalia, and wherever else they stand are testament to our resolve."

Which is more compelling? Interests? Or *Vital* interests?

Diplomacy? Or *peaceful* diplomacy?

Americans? Or *brave* Americans?

And there's an algorithm for quickly adding attached adjectives: Go through your message, underline all the nouns and verbs, and stick a modifying adjective right next to them. (Hint: This is a good opportunity to create some alliterative couplets, fragmented or otherwise). Then, once you've done this, remove the weaker adjectives, leaving only the most eloquent ones.

KEY INSIGHT:

Descriptive Adjectives Call Forth Particular Aspects of the Noun They Describe. (Obviously...)

Not-So-Obviously, This Offers You a Chance to Emphasize the Aspect of the Most Meaning.

PASSAGE #23:

But our greatest strength is the power of our ideas, which are still new in many lands. Across the world, we see them embraced, and we rejoice. Our hopes, our hearts, our hands, are with those on every continent who are building democracy and freedom. Their cause is America's cause.

SECRET #23:

Stacked inclusive pronouns, assonance, consonance, tricolon, fragmented alliteration, reverse fragmented alliteration, strict micro-repetition, asyndeton, strict micro-parallelism, descending / reverse-climax, tiered o-a flow (all in six words, not to mention what I missed)...

All this stuff happens in six words.

The words?

These words: "Our hopes, our hearts, our hands"

Inclusive pronouns are words like "we" or "our" which include the audience in the speaker's message.

He uses stacked inclusive pronouns: "Our... Our... Our..."

He uses assonance, the repetition of vowel sounds: "*Ou*r h*o*pes, *ou*r h*ea*rts, *ou*r h*a*nds" Ou, O, Ou, Ea, Ou, A.

He uses consonance, the repetition of consonant sounds: "Ou*r* *h*ope*s*, ou*r* *h*eart*s*, ou*r* *h*and*s*,"

He uses tricolon: It's a list of three.

He uses fragmented alliteration. In fact, there are two fragmented alliteration paradigms, and they fragment each other: "*O*ur *h*opes, *o*ur *h*earts, *o*ur *h*ands." O, O, O is one; H, H, H is the other: And they fragment each other: O, H, O, H, O, H.

And if two fragmented alliteration paradigms fragmenting each other weren't enough, he uses two *reverse* fragmented alliteration paradigms fragmenting each other: "Ou*r* hope*s*, ou*r* heart*s*, ou*r* hand*s*." R, R, R, S, S, S, fragmenting each other: R, S, R, S, R, S.

He uses strict micro-repetition of "our."

He uses asyndeton, omitting what would have been a grammatically correct "and," creating "our hopes, our hearts, and our hands." Asyndeton, as we discussed, is powerful and eloquent for its own reasons. It's possible he went for asyndeton to maintain the perfection of this sequence, as an "and" would have thrown it off.

It is, of course, strictly micro-parallel.

And he uses descending climax, also known as reverse climax. Climax is arranging ideas in an intensifying or ascending order. Climax is arranging ideas such that whatever quality unites them grows as the communication continues. It typically involves starting with common-place, tangible, concrete ideas and ascending to elevated, existential, and profound ideas of serious consequence.

Reverse climax is the opposite: Arranging them so that they descend, becoming more specific and concrete as the verbal list progresses.

"Our hopes" is more profound, abstract, and elevated than "our hearts," which is more specific and concrete, though still metaphorical. And "our hands" is more specific and concrete, in turn, than "our hearts."

All that in six words. Fascinating.

PASSAGE #24:

The American people have summoned the change we celebrate today. You have raised your voices in an unmistakable chorus. You have cast your votes in historic numbers. And you have changed the face of Congress, the presidency and the political process itself. Yes, you, my fellow Americans have forced the spring. Now, we must do the work the season demands.

SECRET #24:

Strict sentence-level parallelism, stacked.

We've seen micro-parallelism, both strict and loose. We haven't quite focused on sentence-level parallelism yet. And this example happens to be strict sentence-level parallelism, in which the grammatical structures of two entire sentences are identical. (And they are back-to-back sentences, rendering the device stacked).

The two sentences? "You (pronoun) have (auxiliary verb) raised (past-tense verb) your (possessive pronoun) voices (noun) in (preposition) an (article) unmistakable (adjective) chorus (noun). You (pronoun) have (auxiliary verb) cast (past-tense verb) your (possessive pronoun) votes (noun) in (preposition) historic (adjective) numbers (noun)."

Sentence one: Pronoun, auxiliary verb, past-tense verb, possessive pronoun, noun, preposition, article, adjective, noun.

Sentence two: Pronoun, auxiliary verb, past-tense verb, possessive pronoun, noun, preposition, adjective, noun.

Note: It's about the parts of speech, not necessarily their tenses. Mirroring tenses just makes it more strictly parallel, with the symmetry further announcing itself.

And the symmetries go further, though this isn't about parallelism anymore. A compelling one? The two nouns, "voices" and "votes," are alliterative, assonant, consonant, and reverse-alliterative, to name just a few.

PASSAGE #25:

To that work I now turn, with all the authority of my office. I ask the Congress to join with me. But no president, no Congress, no government, can undertake this mission alone. My fellow Americans, you, too, must play your part in our renewal. I challenge a new generation of young Americans to a season of service; to act on your idealism by helping troubled children, keeping company with those in need, reconnecting our torn communities. There is so much to be done; enough indeed for millions of others who are still young in spirit to give of themselves in service, too.

SECRET #25:

Repetitive theme-indicating metaphors.

Remember the discussion of subjects with themes acting as lenses through which to view the subject? And how Clinton spoke about America through the lens of change, frequently repeating the two words "change" and "America" together? Not to mention countless words in the same vein, like frequent repetition of "new."

Now: Clinton, throughout the entire speech, spoke through the metaphor of seasons; specifically, winter turning into spring. This is a theme-indicating metaphor: The flux of seasons acting as an indicator of change, the theme through which Clinton views America. He repeats this metaphor in this passage: "I challenge a *new* generation of young Americans to a *season* of service."

HOW METAPHORS EMPOWER YOUR THEME

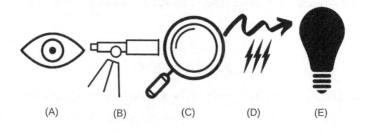

(A)   (B)   (C)   (D)   (E)

FIGURE 17: Using metaphors (B) creates a lens for your lens; a lens for your theme (C). It shapes human perception (A) of your subject (E) to an even higher degree (D).

PASSAGE #26:

In serving, we recognize a simple but powerful truth, we need each other. And we must care for one another. Today, we do more than celebrate America; we rededicate ourselves to the very idea of America.

SECRET #26:

Stacked periodic segments emphasizing one word.

What's a periodic segment? A segment placing its key word or most important idea at its end. And Clinton stacks two such segments in the same sentence, using the "periodic position" to emphasize the same word: "Today, we do more than celebrate *America*; we rededicate ourselves to the very idea of *America*."

Why does this work? Because certain positions in a sentence or segment carry inherent emphasis. Words in those positions rise in perceived importance simply by holding those places of emphasis.

And periodic sentences are eloquent because they don't waste the important position on an unimportant word, instead saving it for a word that deserves to be emphasized. It uses the structure of the language to augment its meaning. And this is a bedrock function of countless secrets of eloquence: generating coherence between the meaning of words and their presentation.

PASSAGE #27:

An idea born in revolution and renewed through two centuries of challenge. An idea tempered by the knowledge that, but for fate we, the fortunate and the unfortunate, might have been each other. An idea ennobled by the faith that our nation can summon from its myriad diversity the deepest measure of unity. An idea infused with the conviction that America's long heroic journey must go forever upward.

SECRET #27:

Double attached adjectives (plus an anaphora paradigm with parallel structures).

You're familiar with attached adjectives. Double attached adjectives elevate a word by using two adjectives to enumerate two of its important characteristics: Compare "America's *long heroic* journey" to "America's long journey" or "America's heroic journey," or even just "America's journey."

It's much more compelling and eloquent.

And this passage also displays an anaphora paradigm leading into sentences with loosely parallel structures: "*An idea* born in revolution and renewed through two centuries of challenge. *An idea* tempered by the knowledge that, but for fate we, the fortunate and the unfortunate, might have been each other. *An idea* ennobled by the faith that our nation can summon from its myriad diversity the deepest measure of unity. *An idea* infused with the conviction that America's long heroic journey must go forever upward."

PASSAGE #28:

And so, my fellow Americans, at the edge of the 21st century, let us begin with energy and hope, with faith and discipline, and let us work until our work is done. The scripture says, "And let us not be weary in well-doing, for in due season, we shall reap, if we faint not."

SECRET #28:

A1, P1, P2, A2 construction.

You know the drill.

A1 introduces the sentence and actions.

P1 introduces the qualities with which the action is conducted.

P2 introduces more qualities with which the action is conducted, in a format parallel to P1 (that's why we call it *P1* and *P2* and not some other letter).

A2 resolves the initial sentence, creating balance and symmetry, sandwiching the P1 and P2 in between A1 and A2.

"And so, my fellow Americans, at the edge of the 21st century, let us begin (A1) with energy and hope (P1), with faith and discipline (P2), and let us work until our work is done (A2)."

PASSAGE #29:

From this joyful mountaintop of celebration, we hear a call to service in the valley. We have heard the trumpets. We have changed the guard. And now, each in our way, and with God's help, we must answer the call. Thank you, and God bless you all.

SECRET #29:

Elevated and figurative language.

Are they really on a joyful mountaintop of celebration? Do they really hear a call to service in the valley? Are there really trumpets, and have they really changed the guard? No. But this passage conveys the power of elevated and figurative language. It certainly made you feel something. And that's eloquence.

...............................Chapter Summary.................................

- Clinton activated the rhyme as reason effect with frequent alliterative couplets.
- Clinton activated the illusory truth effect (repetition raising the perception of accuracy) with many repetitive devices.
- Clinton united the entire speech by speaking through the lens of a metaphor of seasonal change.

- Clinton stacked, layered, nested, and flowed rhetorical devices – these concepts reoccur throughout the book.
- Clinton's "rhetorical density (RD)," the amount of rhetorical artistry divided by number of words, varied.
- Clinton produced very high RD segments, stuffing many devices into six words, but simpler, low RD segments too.

KEY INSIGHT:

The Best Art Conceals Itself. Obvious Rhetoric is Bad Rhetoric. So Too with Rhyme.

Technique and Artistry Can't Stand in the Way of Your Connection to Your Audience.

Email Peter D. Andrei, the author of the Speak for Success collection and the President of Speak Truth Well LLC directly.

pandreibusiness@gmail.com

YOUR RHETORICAL TOOLBOX (PART ONE)

1	Use Clinton's Rhetorical Secrets
1.1	Inclusive Pronouns Establish Empathy and Parity
1.2	Your Subject is What You're Talking About
1.3	Your Lens is the Perspective You Approach the Subject Through
1.4	Alliteration Starts Consecutive Words with the Same Sound
1.5	Alliterative Couples are Two Consecutive Alliterative Words
1.6	Fragmented Alliteration Has Intervening Words Breaking It Up
1.7	Reverse Alliteration Ends Words with the Same Sound
1.8	Tricolons are Lists of Three Creating Compelling Flow and Rhythm
1.9	Nested Rhetorical Devices Occur Within a Dominant Device
1.10	Opposing Structures, Meanings, Words, etc., Create Contrast
1.11	Matching Structures, Meanings, Words, etc., Create Symmetry
1.12	Superabundance is Rhetorical Addition; Expansion; Stretching
1.13	Intensifying Superabundance Adds a Pile of Intense Elaboration
1.14	"Verb-Saturated" Language Delivers Action-Oriented Narrative
1.15	Layered Devices Are of Equal Force and Occur Concurrently
1.16	In- and Out-Flow Occurs When One Word Ends Device A, Starts B
1.17	Fragmented Alliterative Couplets: "Strong and Stable."
1.18	Reverse Fragmented Alliteration: "Fight for What is Right."
1.19	Enumeratio Breaks Up an Item into its Constituent Parts

1.20	Assonance Repeats Vowel Sounds in Close Proximity
1.21	Consonance Repeats Consonant Sounds in Close Proximity
1.22	Parallelism Occurs When Segments Share Grammatical Structure
1.23	Loose Parallelism Occurs When Segments Only Share Grammar
1.24	Front-Back Alliteration: "Strong, Fast"
1.25	Phonetically Undone Couplet: Two Phonetics Undoing Each Other
1.26	Action-Oriented Language Creates a Self-Driven Narrative
1.27	Strict Parallelism is Identical Grammar and Some Word Repetition
1.28	Strictly Parallel Tricolon: Three Comma-Split Strict Parallels
1.29	Asyndeton Omits Grammatically Accurate Conjunctions
1.30	Pattern-Interrupts Break Away from a Preceding Pattern
1.31	Micro Devices Occur on Small Scales: Letters and Words
1.32	Macro Devices Occur on Large Scales: Paragraphs and Passages
1.33	X, X, YX Pattern-Interrupts: "From Time to Time... Our Time."
1.34	Simple Contrast: Two Contrasting Words in Close Proximity
1.35	Anaphora Starts Subsequent Sentences with the Same Words
1.36	Anaphora Paradigms are Anaphora-Based Structural Segments
1.37	Fragmented Anaphora Paradigms Have Intervening Material
1.38	X, YX Pattern-Interrupts: "It Can Be Done, and Done Fairly."
1.39	Stacked Pattern Interrupts Stack Pattern-Breaking Strategies

1.40	A, B1X, C1Y, D1Z Constructions: "For X, From X, To X"
1.41	Micro-Parallelism is Word or Segment-Level Parallelism
1.42	Stacked Micro-Parallelism Stacks Micro-Parallel Segments
1.43	Noun Couplets Emphasize an Item by Using Two Words for it
1.44	Stacked Contrasts Stack Contrasting Phrases Together
1.45	Symmetrical Word Choice Creates Rhetorical Unity
1.46	Inundating Contrasts Creates a "Superabundance" of Contrast
1.47	"While" Constructions Transition and Create Narrative Movement
1.48	Attached Adjectives Modify Directly Subsequent Nouns
1.49	Climax Arranges Items in Order of Increasing Intensity
1.50	Reverse Climax Arranges Items in Order of Decreasing Intensity
1.51	Letter-Level Flow: Rhetorical Symmetry at the Smallest Level
1.52	Tiered O-A Flow: A Particular Form of Letter-Level Flow
1.53	Themes Are Perspectives Through Which to View a Subject
1.54	Metaphors Equate Two Items
1.55	Theme-Indicating Metaphors Compare the Theme to Something
1.56	Rhetorical Emphasis Uses Components of Rhetoric to Emphasize
1.57	Periodic Sentences Place the Key Word in the Final Position
1.58	Stacked Periodic Segments Sequence Periodic Segments
1.59	Double Attached Adjectives: "America's Long Heroic Journey..."

1.60	A1, P1, P2, A2: "Let Us X with Y, with Z, and Let Us J"
1.61	Elevated and Figurative Language Uses Non-Pedestrian Words
2	Use Reagan's Rhetorical Secrets
3	Use JFK's Rhetorical Secrets

KEY INSIGHT:

Knowing Rhetorical Devices Supplies Your Subconscious Mind with Frameworks.

When It Sees an Opportunity to Use These Frameworks, It Throws an "Inspiration" Into Your Conscious Awareness.

"This is a Great Place for Anaphora. Use This Nice Alliterative Couplet."

BILL CLINTON'S SENSORY LANGUAGE

👁 *From this joyful mountaintop of celebration....*

🔊 *we hear a call to service...*

👁 *in the valley.*

🔊 *We have heard the trumpets.*

👁 *We have changed the guard.*

Claim These Free Resources that Will Help You Unleash the Power of Your Words and Speak with Confidence. Visit www.speakforsuccesshub.com/toolkit for Access.

18 Free PDF Resources

12 Iron Rules for Captivating Story, 21 Speeches that Changed the World, 341-Point Influence Checklist, 143 Persuasive Cognitive Biases, 17 Ways to Think On Your Feet, 18 Lies About Speaking Well, 137 Deadly Logical Fallacies, 12 Iron Rules For Captivating Slides, 371 Words that Persuade, 63 Truths of Speaking Well, 27 Laws of Empathy, 21 Secrets of Legendary Speeches, 19 Scripts that Persuade, 12 Iron Rules For Captivating Speech, 33 Laws of Charisma, 11 Influence Formulas, 219-Point Speech-Writing Checklist, 21 Eloquence Formulas

Claim These Free Resources that Will Help You Unleash the Power of Your Words and Speak with Confidence. Visit www.speakforsuccesshub.com/toolkit for Access.

30 Free Video Lessons

We'll send you one free video lesson every day for 30 days, written and recorded by Peter D. Andrei. Days 1-10 cover authenticity, the prerequisite to confidence and persuasive power. Days 11-20 cover building self-belief and defeating communication anxiety. Days 21-30 cover how to speak with impact and influence, ensuring your words change minds instead of falling flat. Authenticity, self-belief, and impact – this course helps you master three components of confidence, turning even the most high-stakes presentations from obstacles into opportunities.

Claim These Free Resources that Will Help You Unleash the Power of Your Words and Speak with Confidence. Visit www.speakforsuccesshub.com/toolkit for Access.

2 Free Workbooks

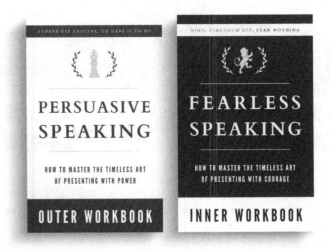

We'll send you two free workbooks, including long-lost excerpts by Dale Carnegie, the mega-bestselling author of *How to Win Friends and Influence People* (5,000,000 copies sold). *Fearless Speaking* guides you in the proven principles of mastering your inner game as a speaker. *Persuasive Speaking* guides you in the time-tested tactics of mastering your outer game by maximizing the power of your words. All of these resources complement the Speak for Success collection.

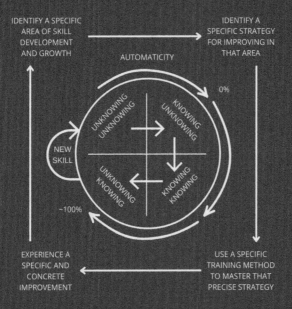

How do anxious speakers turn into articulate masters of the craft? Here's how: With the bulletproof, scientifically-proven, 2,500-year-old (but mostly forgotten) process pictured above.

First, we identify a specific area of improvement. Perhaps your body language weakens your connection with the audience. At this point, you experience "unknowing unknowing." You don't know you don't know the strategy you will soon learn for improving in this area.

Second, we choose a specific strategy for improving in this area. Perhaps we choose "open gestures," a type of gesturing that draws the audience in and holds attention.

At this point, you experience "knowing unknowing." You know you don't know the strategy. Your automaticity, or how automatically you perform the strategy when speaking, is 0%.

Third, we choose a specific drill or training method to help you practice open gestures. Perhaps you give practice speeches and perform the gestures. At this point, you experience "knowing knowing." You know you know the strategy.

And through practice, you formed a weak habit, so your automaticity is somewhere between 0% and 100%.

Fourth, you continue practicing the technique. You shift into "unknowing knowing." You forgot you use this type of gesture, because it became a matter of automatic habit. Your automaticity is 100%.

And just like that, you've experienced a significant and concrete improvement. You've left behind a weakness in communication and gained a strength. Forever. Every time you speak, you use this type of gesture, and you do it without even thinking about it. This alone can make the difference between a successful and unsuccessful speech.

Now repeat. Master a new skill. Create a new habit. Improve in a new area. How else could we improve your body language? What about the structure of your communication? Your persuasive strategy? Your debate skill? Your vocal modulation? With this process, people gain measurable and significant improvements in as little as one hour. Imagine if you stuck with it over time. This is the path to mastery. This is the path to unleashing the power of your words.

Access your 18 free PDF resources, 30 free video lessons, and 2 free workbooks from this link: www.speakforsuccesshub.com/toolkit

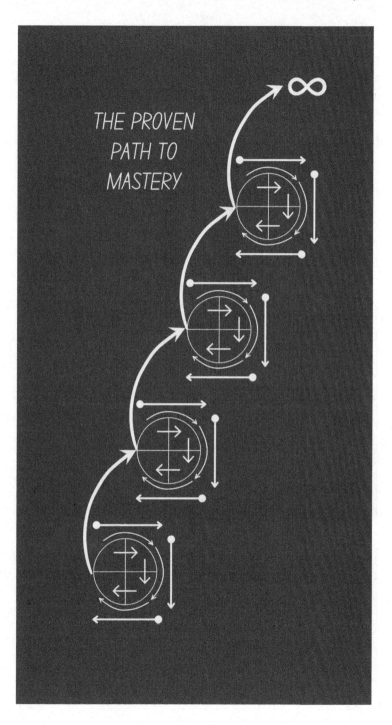

SPEAK FOR SUCCESS COLLECTION BOOK

II

ELOQUENCE CHAPTER

III

THE SECOND SPEECH:
Ronald Reagan's Inaugural Address

"NOTHING LESS THAN A MIRACLE..."

RONALD REAGAN DELIVERED THIS address on January 20, 1981. It paints a picture at once urgent and inspirational; antagonistic and conciliatory; relatively easy-going and yet eminently eloquent. His distinct style shines through, as it always should. He casts a reformist vision, offering a reversal of the policies of prior presidents flowing from his conservative ideology. Let us begin.

PASSAGE #1:

Senator Hatfield, Mr. Chief Justice, Mr. President, Vice President Bush, Vice President Mondale, Senator Baker, Speaker O'Neill, Reverend Moomaw, and my fellow citizens: To a few of us here today this is a solemn and most momentous occasion, and yet in the history of our nation it is a commonplace occurrence. The orderly transfer of authority as called for in the Constitution routinely takes place, as it has for almost two centuries, and few of us stop to think how unique we really are. In the eyes of many in the world, this every-four-year ceremony we accept as normal is nothing less than a miracle.

SECRET #30:

Implicit micro-repetition.

We talked about strict micro-repetition. And I told you there are many other modes of repetition. Well, here's one: *Implicit* micro-repetition. How does it work? It repeats the same sentiment, stacking together words suggesting the same idea.

Why is this good? Because it subtly and subconsciously reinforces the sentiment in people's minds.

"To a few of us here today this is a solemn and most momentous occasion, and yet in the history of our nation it is a *commonplace* occurrence. The orderly transfer of authority as called for in the Constitution *routinely* takes place, as it has for *almost two centuries*, and few of us stop to think how unique we really are. In the eyes of many in the world, this *every-four-year* ceremony we accept as *normal* is nothing less than a miracle."

THE PSYCHOLOGY OF COMPELLING REPETITION

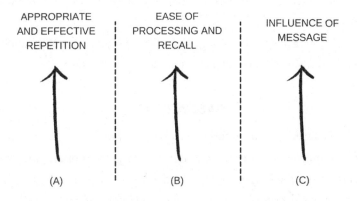

FIGURE 18: As you use repetition appropriately and effectively (A), the ease of processing and recall (B) rises, which increases the influence of your message (C) by activating a complex bundle of biases and heuristics.

PASSAGE #2:

Mr. President, I want our fellow citizens to know how much you did to carry on this tradition. By your gracious cooperation in the transition process, you have shown a watching world that we are a united people pledged to maintaining a political system which guarantees individual liberty to a greater degree than any other, and I thank you and your people for all your help in maintaining the continuity which is the bulwark of our Republic.

SECRET #31:

Alliterative couplet with an attached adjective.

We discussed, briefly, how the algorithm through which you can apply attached adjectives is a fast and easy way to introduce some alliterative couplets too, simply by choosing an adjective starting with the same letter as the word it modifies and sits next to (or another nearby word).

This creates the following effect: "By your gracious cooperation in the transition process, you have shown a *watching world...*"

PASSAGE #3:

The business of our nation goes forward. These United States are confronted with an economic affliction of great proportions. We suffer from the longest and one of the worst sustained inflations in our national history. It distorts our economic decisions, penalizes thrift, and crushes the struggling young and the fixed-income elderly alike. It threatens to shatter the lives of millions of our people.

SECRET #32:

The example triad.

Lists of three are extremely appealing to human beings. Three items are the smallest number of items necessary for creating a pattern that announces itself to human perception. Lists of three are, for myriad reasons, inherently intuitive to the human mind. And Reagan uses a simple strategy for introducing a list of three in his language: "We suffer from the longest and one of the worst sustained inflations in our national history. *It distorts our economic decisions, penalizes thrift, and crushes the struggling young and the fixed-income elderly alike.*"

The basic formula is (claim), (example / expansion one), (example / expansion two), (example / expansion three).

THE EXAMPLE TRIAD VISUALIZED

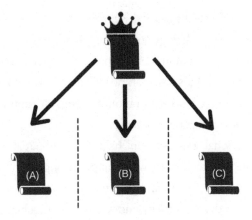

FIGURE 19: Make a claim. Provide three examples. Move on. It's that simple. The example triad is one of the simplest and most versatile eloquence algorithms.

The list of three carries tremendous persuasive weight and sounds eloquent and attractive. And you can apply example triads by a similar algorithm as the one you used to apply attached adjectives. Highlight all your claims, and infuse an example triad in its own sentence following each claim, or for however many claims you see fit. Then, keep the effective ones while sculpting away the weak ones.

PASSAGE #4:

Idle industries have cast workers into unemployment, human misery, and personal indignity. Those who do work are denied a fair return for their labor by a tax system which penalizes successful achievement and keeps us from maintaining full productivity.

SECRET #33:

Emotionally triggering words.

We, as human beings, over the course of our evolution, developed an innate and immensely powerful emotional algorithm. It's inescapable. And it's based on two pillars: Positive emotions and negative emotions. Positive emotions suggest approach, and negative emotions suggest avoidance.

This emotional "radar system" helped keep us out of trouble tens of thousands of years ago when approaching a threat in the wilderness could spell a fast and gruesome death.

What does this mean? How does this produce eloquence? And how does Reagan use it? It's simple: An essential element of eloquence is engagement. What do I mean by engagement? I mean that properly eloquent language practically forces listeners to intellectually and emotionally engage. They can't avoid it.

Using emotionally triggering words produces engagement, and thus eloquence, by appealing to this internal, 2,000,000-year-old emotional metronome we all have buried deep in our psyches.

Reagan uses words triggering avoidance emotions: Avoidance of the alternative to his presidency, which his presidency will supposedly save the public from.

"*Idle* industries have *cast* workers into *unemployment*, human *misery*, and personal *indignity*."

Because these words trigger a visceral emotional reaction, they engage. Thus, they are eloquent.

PASSAGE #5:

But great as our tax burden is, it has not kept pace with public spending. For decades we have piled deficit upon deficit, mortgaging our future and our children's future for the temporary convenience of the present. To continue this long trend is to guarantee tremendous social, cultural, political, and economic upheavals.

SECRET #34:

Sententia.

Sententia summarizes preceding material in a simple, short, punchy sentence: "To continue this long trend is to guarantee tremendous social, cultural, political, and economic upheavals."

A powerful algorithm for developing a sententia statement is asking, "Yes, and?" until the question seems ridiculous when stacked against the self-evidence of the answer. "But great as our tax burden is, it has not kept pace with public spending. *(Yes, and?)* For decades we have piled deficit upon deficit *(Yes, and?)*, mortgaging our future and our children's future for the temporary convenience of the present. *(Yes, and?)* To continue this long trend is to guarantee tremendous social, cultural, political, and economic upheavals *(Sententia – asking 'yes, and?' just sounds silly at this point)*."

WHY SENTENTIA MAKES YOUR MESSAGE MEMORABLE

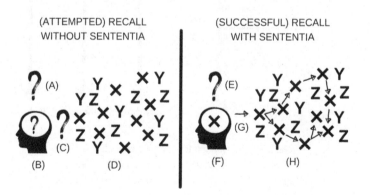

FIGURE 20: Human memory functions in part through associative cascades: a question triggers an associated

memory, which triggers a "shotgun scatter" of associative memories. The strength of this associative network contributes to the strength of one's memory. Without sententia, the question or prompt (A) doesn't trigger any immediate associations (B) which doesn't provide a link (C) to the memory ensemble (D). As a result, there is no recall of the message. With sententia, however, the prompt (E) quickly triggers recollection of the sententia statement (F), which links to the memory ensemble (G) and triggers the associative cascade (H), resulting in much higher recall of the overall message. As a result, the sententia statement acts as a stepping-stone to complete recall. Without the sententia statement (or any other strategy serving the same function), it is like trying to climb a ladder with the first eight rungs missing. Sure, some people may be able to. Most people will not. The sententia statement acts like a fourth rung on the ladder, helping people make the journey up toward complete (or at least more complete) recall.

GENERATING AN ELECTRICIFYING SENTENTIA STATEMENT

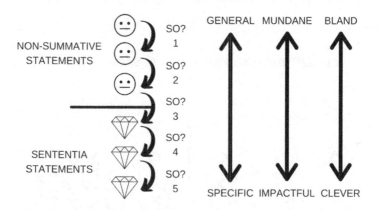

FIGURE 21: The algorithm for finding a powerful sententia statement is starting with the content you wish to link to a sententia, and asking questions designed to dig deep at its most fundamental impact. Ask "yes, and?" or "so?" a number of times. Each time you do, the statement becomes more specific and impactful, and oftentimes cleverer as well. These qualities make for a compelling

sententia statement. Remember to keep the sententia statement short. It is a summary; a signpost. It is a guide to the complete message; it is not the complete message. It captures the bare essence of the complete message.

PASSAGE #6:

You and I, as individuals, can, by borrowing, live beyond our means, but for only a limited period of time. Why, then, should we think that collectively, as a nation, we're not bound by that same limitation? We must act today in order to preserve tomorrow. And let there be no misunderstanding: We are going to begin to act, beginning today.

SECRET #35:

Analogy, rhetorical question, micro repetition, and frontloaded transitions.

I just said it: Eloquent language produces engagement. And complicated subject matter tends to disengage for myriad psychological reasons we won't get into now. Thus, eloquent language is simple. It's beautiful, perhaps for complex reasons (as you know by now), but it remains simple to hear and receive.

Analogies simplify a complicated idea by comparing it to a familiar and simple one. And thus, analogies produce eloquent language. Here's how Reagan uses an analogy: "You and I, as individuals, can, by borrowing, live beyond our means, but for only a limited period of time. Why, then, should we think that collectively, as a nation, we're not bound by that same limitation?"

And this also presents a rhetorical question, which is extremely eloquent because it produces engagement, creating intellectual interaction with the subject matter. They are also persuasive because, in trying to answer the question (which human minds will do automatically), people will come to the inevitable answer, thus realizing the speaker's point themselves, from within, instead of having it hammered into their heads from without.

There's more micro-repetition, both implicit and strict: "We must *act today* in order to preserve tomorrow. And let there be no misunderstanding: We are going to *begin* to *act, beginning today*."

Finally, frontloaded transitions: "And let there be no misunderstanding..." Frontloaded transitions precede the sentence, maintaining attention and carrying it over from a previous sentence instead of losing it. How? By giving people an intellectual directive with which to receive the coming meaning.

PASSAGE #7:

The economic ills we suffer have come upon us over several decades. They will not go away in days, weeks, or months, but they will go away. They will go away because we as Americans have the capacity now, as we've had in the past, to do whatever needs to be done to preserve this last and greatest bastion of freedom.

SECRET #36:

N1, N1A, N1B, N1C, Y1 constructions.

Another one of these. Fun, aren't they? (I think so).

Let's break it down...

N1: "They will not go away..."

N1A "in days..."

N1B "weeks..."

N1C "or months..."

Y1: "but they will go away..."

N1: What won't happen in particular ways?

N1A: What's one of the particular ways in which it won't happen?

N1B: What's another one of the particular ways in which it won't happen?

N1C: What's another one of the particular ways in which it won't happen?"

Y1: But what will still happen? (N for no, Y for yes).

KEY INSIGHT:

Individual Examples of Eloquent Sentence Structures Are Less Important Than What They Reveal: That Eloquent Sentence Structures with Inherent Balance, Appeal, and Impact Exist.

PASSAGE #8:

In this present crisis, government is not the solution to our problem; government is the problem. From time to time we've been tempted to believe that society has become too complex to be managed by self-rule, that government by an elite group is superior to government for, by, and of the people. Well, if no one among us is capable of governing himself, then who among us has the capacity to govern someone else? All of us together, in and out of government, must bear the burden. The solutions we seek must be equitable, with no one group singled out to pay a higher price.

SECRET #37:

Reframing: "(noun one) is not (noun two), but (opposite of noun two)."

A frame is an established relationship between two items, acting as a foundational assumption and subtle starting point in discussions about a subject: "X is Y."

Who established it? Nobody knows. Maybe your interlocuter. Or maybe it's a long-standing assumption. Regardless, reframing is the art of taking the preexisting assumption and, if it doesn't work for your rhetorical goals, rearranging it. And there are several specific reframing rearrangements producing the image of insight. We'll talk about the one Reagan used: *Second item reversal.*

The initial frame was "government is the solution." ("X is Y" is the basic formula allowing us to easily conceptualize a frame, and even if the frame is worded differently, the exact same meaning can be arranged to fit this formula).

Reagan discounted the initial frame in the first half of an antithesis structure. Antithesis is uniquely suited to reframing, taking the form "not X, but Y." Reagan said "government is not the solution (X)..." Then, he presented the reframe: "...government is the problem (Y)."

The basic structure is as follows: "X is not Y; X is Z," where Z is the opposite of Y. And why does it work? Because it is innately, intrinsically, inherently intuitive. Reversing the intellectual status quo with this mode of reframing appears clairvoyant and produces eloquent language.

PASSAGE #9:

We hear much of special interest groups. Well, our concern must be for a special interest group that has been too long neglected. It knows no sectional boundaries or ethnic and racial divisions, and it crosses political party lines. It is made up of men and women who raise our food, patrol our streets, man our mines and factories, teach our children, keep our homes, and heal us when we're sick – professionals, industrialists, shopkeepers, clerks, cabbies, and truckdrivers. They are, in short, "We the people," this breed called Americans.

SECRET #38:

Parallel enumeratio and breakaway phrases.

We discussed enumeratio. This passage layers parallelism over enumeratio, and stacks short, parallel segments together in an immensely eloquent sequence.

"It is made up of men and women who raise (verb) our food (noun), patrol (verb) our streets (noun), man (verb) our mines and factories (noun couplet), teach our children (noun), keep (verb) our homes (noun), and heal us when we're sick (breakaway phrase)."

As you can see, it is parallel in the form "(verb) our (noun)." And through repeating this parallel structure, it establishes a pattern, which builds a slightly tense and staccato rhythm gently resolved by the breakaway phrase (which also grabs attention because it breaks a pattern). Supremely eloquent.

PASSAGE #10:

Well, this administration's objective will be a healthy, vigorous, growing economy that provides equal opportunities for all Americans with no barriers born of bigotry or discrimination. Putting America back to work means putting all Americans back to work.

Ending inflation means freeing all Americans from the terror of runaway living costs. All must share in the productive work of this "new beginning," and all must share in the bounty of a revived economy. With the idealism and fair play which are the core of our system and our strength, we can have a strong and prosperous America, at peace with itself and the world.

SECRET #39:

Alliteration, consonance, and assonance layered over each other with in-flow and out-flow.

It might sound, based on the heading, like this secret manifests itself throughout an entire passage. Not so: Just six words. The six words? "Barriers born of bigotry or discrimination."

The alliteration in the sentence? "*B*arriers *b*orn of *b*igotry or discrimination."

The consonance? (Of course, alliteration technically produces consonance, so we'll ignore the "b" consonance): "Ba*rr*ie*r*s bo*rn* of bigot*ry* o*r* disc*r*imination."

And what about the assonance? "Barr*ie*rs b*o*rn *o*f big*o*tr*y (this y sounds like the ie in barriers – assonance regards sounds, not letters) o*r* d*i*scr*imi*nat*io*n*.*" There are two assonance paradigms here. More on this shortly.

These devices twist in and out of each other. They are layered with in-flow and out-flow. They are nested within each other, but also flow in and out of each other as certain words mark the end of one paradigm and the continuation of another (like bigotry, which ends the alliterative paradigm and continues the assonance of "o").

RHETORICAL IN- AND OUT-FLOW VISUALIZED

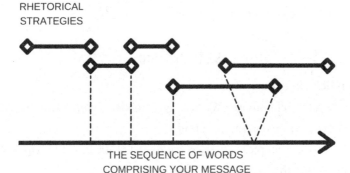

RHETORICAL
STRATEGIES

THE SEQUENCE OF WORDS
COMPRISING YOUR MESSAGE

FIGURE 22: Rhetorical in-flow and out-flow occurs when the end of a rhetorical strategy or rhetorical paradigm (like anaphora, assonance, consonance, alliteration, parallelism) overlaps with the beginning of another one. The dotted lines indicate where in-flow and out-flow occur in this abstracted sequence of rhetorical strategies.

And it gets more interesting: Assonance can have in-flow and out-flow with assonance. And the same goes for consonance and alliteration: They can flow in and out of themselves.

How? Pay attention to this: "Barriers born of bigotry or discrimination."

BArrEErs bOrn Of bIgOtREE Or dIscrImInAtIOn.

A, EE, O, O, I, O, EE, O, I, I, I, A, IO: O assonance is nested within EE assonance, which ends while the O assonance flows into I assonance (which seems to "call back" to the I in "bigotry"), which flows into loose A assonance (bArriers ... discriminAtion).

PASSAGE #11:

So, as we begin, let us take inventory. We are a nation that has a government – not the other way around. And this makes us special among the nations of the Earth. Our government has no power except that granted it by the people. It is time to check and reverse the growth of government, which shows signs of having grown beyond the consent of the governed.

SECRET #40:

Implicit chiasmus.

What's chiasmus? Words, grammatical constructions, or concepts repeated in reverse order.

A good example? "Poetry is the record of the best and happiest moments of the happiest and best minds."

And this passage by Reagan implies chiasmus. How? When he says "We are a nation that has a government – not the other way around…" the natural mental response by the audience is to mentally specify his meaning: "We are a nation that has a government… not a government that has a nation." (I would have actually said this if I were Reagan – don't you agree that it's better?)

Now: It's not certain everyone at all times would complete the chiasmus in their own heads. But many likely would. And this is an unparalleled level of eloquence: Providing the audience the ingredients to conclude eloquent language in their own heads.

The phrase "…not the other way around," on its own, means nothing. It calls for a rearrangement of the preceding material. And Reagan doesn't provide it. Instead, he allows the minds of his listeners to generate it, making this intellectually interactive and captivating as a result.

PASSAGE #12:

It is my intention to curb the size and influence of the Federal establishment and to demand recognition of the distinction between the powers granted to the Federal Government and those reserved to the States or to the people. All of us need to be reminded that the Federal Government did not create the States; the States created the Federal Government.

SECRET #41:

Explicit chiasmus.

Amazing: We just discussed implicit chiasmus, and right here, in the next passage, Reagan uses explicit chiasmus.

Coincidence? Not really.

Why not? Because an effective message creates the correct emotions in the audience, and in the correct sequence. Different rhetorical devices belong to different categories which create certain effects on the audience. See the logical conclusion of this?

Reagan uses chiasmus here twice, and infrequently in the rest of the speech because here, at this point, he can serve his purpose by creating the particular emotion chiasmus spawns: A feeling of epiphany and enlightenment.

"Government did not create the States; the States created the Federal Government." It's also reframing.

PASSAGE #13:

Now, so there will be no misunderstanding, it's not my intention to do away with government. It is rather to make it work – work with us, not over us; to stand by our side, not ride on our back. Government can and must provide opportunity, not smother it; foster productivity, not stifle it.

SECRET #42:

Stacked reversed antitheticals: "do this, not that" four times.

An antithetical is "not X, but Y." A reversed antithetical is "X, not Y." And in this passage, Reagan stacks four such constructions.

"It is rather to make it work – work with us (X), not over us (not Y); to stand by our side (X), not ride on our back (not Y). Government can and must provide opportunity (X), not smother it (not Y); foster productivity (X), not stifle it (not Y)."

PASSAGE #14:

If we look to the answer as to why for so many years we achieved so much, prospered as no other people on Earth, it was because here in this land we unleashed the energy and individual genius of man to a greater extent than has ever been done before. Freedom and the dignity of the individual have been more available and assured here than in any other place on Earth. The price for this freedom at times has been high, but we have never been unwilling to pay that price.

SECRET #43:

Sentence-intervened repetition.

"The price for this freedom at times has been high, but we have never been unwilling to pay that price."

He repeats the word "price" at the start of the sentence as the first word except for the article "the" and at the end.

What does this do? It creates the sense that the sentence is self-resolving: That it's a "question and an answer," coming full circle. This is a necessary component of melody in music: Resolution, often by ending a melody how it began.

PASSAGE #15:

It is no coincidence that our present troubles parallel and are proportionate to the intervention and intrusion in our lives that result from unnecessary and excessive growth of government. It is time for us to realize that we're too great a nation to limit ourselves to small dreams. We're not, as some would have us believe, doomed to an inevitable decline. I do not believe in a fate that will fall on us no matter what we do. I do believe in a fate that will fall on us if we do nothing. So, with all the creative energy at our command, let us begin an era of national renewal. Let us renew our determination, our courage, and our strength. And let us renew our faith and our hope.

SECRET #44:

NA1, YA2 construction.

I want to turn your attention to this pair of sentences: "I do not (N) believe in a fate that will fall on us (A) no matter what we do (1). I do (Y) believe in a fate that will fall on us (A) if we do nothing (2)."

The basic structure is this: "I don't believe X will happen no matter what we do. I do believe X will happen if we do nothing."

An immensely persuasive structure designed to inspire an audience to adopt a solution to a problem is the Problem, Agitate, Solution structure.

Outline a problem. Emotionally agitate the problem. Then present your proposed solution. If you look at passages in both Clinton and Reagan's inaugurals, you'll see this structure clear as day. But many people make one common mistake: eroding belief.

What do I mean by that? They drive the problem home so hard that the endeavor of solving it seems hopeless. But with a language pattern like the one we just uncovered, you can reinforce belief in the possibility of a solution, even for the direst of problems.

PASSAGE #16:

We have every right to dream heroic dreams. Those who say that we're in a time when there are not heroes, they just don't know where to look. You can see heroes every day going in and out of factory gates. Others, a handful in number, produce enough food to feed all of us and then the world beyond. You meet heroes across a counter, and they're on both sides of that counter. There are entrepreneurs with faith in themselves and faith in an idea who create new jobs, new wealth and opportunity. They're individuals and families whose taxes support the government and whose voluntary gifts support church, charity, culture, art, and education. Their patriotism is quiet, but deep. Their values sustain our national life.

SECRET #45:

Conduplicatio.

Conduplicatio is the ancient term for strict repetition, but specifically strict repetition across clauses, segments, or sentences. And we see it in this passage with the repetition of the word "heroes."

But what does it do? What is the rhetorical effect? Why is it eloquent? And when should you use it in your communication?

It achieves amplification, emphasizing a particular idea or theme. And that's the power of all things related to repetition.

RHETORICAL IN-FLOW AND OUT-FLOW VISUALIZED

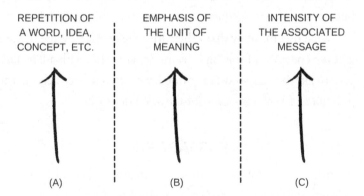

REPETITION OF A WORD, IDEA, CONCEPT, ETC.	EMPHASIS OF THE UNIT OF MEANING	INTENSITY OF THE ASSOCIATED MESSAGE
(A)	(B)	(C)

FIGURE 23: As you repeat a word, idea, or concept, the emphasis placed on it rises, as does the intensity of the message associated with it.

KEY INSIGHT:

If You Have an Important Point to Make, Don't Try to Be Subtle or Clever. Use a Pile Driver. Hit the Point Once. Then Come Back & Hit it Again. – Churchill Conduplicatio Does Exactly That: Hits, Hits, Hits, And Hits Again.

PASSAGE #17:

Now, I have used the words "they" and "their" in speaking of these heroes. I could say "you" and "your," because I'm addressing the heroes of whom I speak – you, the citizens of this blessed land. Your dreams, your hopes, your goals are going to be the dreams, the hopes, and the goals of this administration, so help me God.

SECRET #46:

A1, A2, A3, B1, B2, B3, C construction.
   A1: "Your dreams."
   A2: "Your hopes."
   A3: "Your goals."
   B1: "The dreams."

B2: "The hopes."

B3: "The goals."

C: "Of this administration."

PASSAGE #18:

We shall reflect the compassion that is so much a part of your makeup. How can we love our country and not love our countrymen; and loving them, reach out a hand when they fall, heal them when they're sick, and provide opportunity to make them self-sufficient so they will be equal in fact and not just in theory?

SECRET #47:

Loose anadiplosis, enveloped phonetic repetition.

Anadiplosis is repeating the last word of one segment as the first word of the following segment.

Loose anadiplosis is repeating one of the last words of a segment as one of the first words of the following segments. Reagan uses it as follows: "How can we love our country and not *love* our countrymen; and *loving* them..."

It creates flow, continuity, and rhythm, carrying attention throughout a sequence instead of losing it.

Now: Enveloped phonetic repetition is a drastically sophisticated strategy. It grabs immediate attention like nothing else. What is it? Repeating the *sound* of an entire word without repeating the word.

"How can we love our *country* and not love our *country*men."

Another example is when JFK said, of the poor, that we should "help them help themselves."

"Help them help themselves."

PASSAGE #19:

Can we solve the problems confronting us? Well, the answer is an unequivocal and emphatic "yes." To paraphrase Winston Churchill, I did not take the oath I've just taken with the intention of presiding over the dissolution of the world's strongest economy.

SECRET #48:

Hypophora and open loops.

Curiosity is innate. It is irresistible. It is immensely powerful. And through it, you can command complete attention at any time under any circumstances and against any distractions.

What's a powerful way to arouse curiosity? By creating an open loop. What's that? An unanswered question, causing people to want to close the loop and find an answer. Rhetorical questions are inherently eloquent on their own, but you can use them to arouse curiosity for even more rhetorical benefit.

How? With the rhetorical technique of hypophora: Asking a question, and then answering it. Who, after hearing the speech preceding this, and the problems it outlined, could hear, "Can we solve the problems confronting us?" and not immediately pay attention?

PASSAGE #20:

In the days ahead I will propose removing the roadblocks that have slowed our economy and reduced productivity. Steps will be taken aimed at restoring the balance between the various levels of government. Progress may be slow, measured in inches and feet, not miles, but we will progress. It is time to reawaken this industrial giant, to get government back within its means, and to lighten our punitive tax burden. And these will be our first priorities, and on these principles there will be no compromise.

SECRET #49:

Metaphor.

In this passage, Reagan uses physical distance – "inches and feet, not miles" – as a metric for a measurement it can't actually describe.

And it works. Because his meaning is made vivid, clear, and engaging. Understand: The human mind is designed by 200,000 (or arguably many more) years of evolution to conserve attention, expending mental calories only on what will help someone survive and thrive.

If language is too abstract and difficult to grasp, the mind will stop trying to understand it and disengage. Why? Because the caloric expenditure is too high for too little perceived reward. And eloquence, as you know, is the result of engagement. No engagement? No eloquence.

So, by using simple metaphors like Reagan, you can immediately simplify concepts and maintain command of the audience's attention, achieving eloquence in the process.

PASSAGE #21:

On the eve of our struggle for independence a man who might have been one of the greatest among the Founding Fathers, Dr. Joseph Warren, president of the Massachusetts Congress, said to his fellow Americans, "Our country is in danger, but not to be despaired of... On you depend the fortunes of America. You are to decide the important questions upon which rests the happiness and the liberty of millions yet unborn. Act worthy of yourselves."

SECRET #50:

Borrowed eloquence.

It's simple, and self-evident in this passage: Know of an exceptionally fitting and eloquent quote about your subject? Can you think of a natural way to work it into your communication? And is the speaker someone with personal ethos – that is, credibility – on the matter at hand? Then you can borrow its eloquence by quoting it. Just like Reagan did when he quoted Dr. Joseph Warren.

PASSAGE #22:

Well, I believe we, the Americans of today, are ready to act worthy of ourselves, ready to do what must be done to ensure happiness and liberty for ourselves, our children, and our children's children. And as we renew ourselves here in our own land, we will be seen as having greater strength throughout the world. We will again be the exemplar of freedom and a beacon of hope for those who do not now have freedom.

SECRET #51:

Personal style and universal themes.

I want to draw your attention to the difference in Clinton and Reagan's personal styles. They both speak in an elevated way, carrying tremendous gravitas with their communication. But it seems like Reagan tends to be more conversational at times. What does this have to do with eloquence? Let me explain...

Everyone has a personal style. Yes: Every situation calls for a different mode of communication. But you must not morph yourself so much that you lose the hint of what makes you, well, you; the natural elements of your communication uniquely you and uniquely eloquent when delivered by you.

While the two have slightly different personal styles, they both seem to speak to similar themes at times. Why? Because these emotionally idealized themes appeal to something inherent about what it means to be human; elements of the human psyche buried deep in our neurobiology and evolutionary history.

Just in this last passage, we can see Reagan appealing to several of these universal themes: themes Clinton appealed to as well. And Reagan does it not because Clinton does it, but because they both understand the power of these universal concepts.

The themes? "Well, I believe we, the Americans of today, are ready to act worthy of ourselves, ready to *do what must be done* to ensure *happiness and liberty* for *ourselves, our children, and our children's children.* And as we *renew* ourselves here in our own land, we will be seen as having *greater strength throughout the world.* We will again be the exemplar of *freedom* and a beacon of *hope* for *those who do not now have freedom.*

I'll leave it as an exercise to you to identify Clinton's invocation of these themes. If you want a challenge, try to do it from memory.

PASSAGE #23:

To those neighbors and allies who share our freedom, we will strengthen our historic ties and assure them of our support and firm commitment. We will match loyalty with loyalty. We will strive for mutually beneficial relations. We will not use our friendship to impose on their sovereignty, for our own sovereignty is not for sale. As for the enemies of freedom, those who are potential adversaries, they will be reminded that peace is the highest aspiration of the American people. We will negotiate for it, sacrifice for it; we will not surrender for it, now or ever.

SECRET #52:

Stacked reverse antithesis: "X, Y, not Z."

Antithesis is a "not X, but Y" construction, most famously used here: "We choose to go to the moon in this decade and do the other things, not because they are easy, but because they are hard..."

Reverse antithesis flips it: "Y, not X..."

And stacked antithesis adds components to it: "not X, not Y, not (...) but Z." Reversed, it's "X, Y (...), not Z."

"We will negotiate for it (X), sacrifice for it (Y), not surrender for it (not Z), now or ever."

PASSAGE #24:

Our forbearance should never be misunderstood. Our reluctance for conflict should not be misjudged as a failure of will. When action is required to preserve our national security, we will act. We will maintain sufficient strength to prevail if need be, knowing that if we do so we have the best chance of never having to use that strength.

SECRET #53:

Varied sentence length.

Remember: Eloquence engages. And patterns habituate over time, slowly sliding out of our perception. That which we don't perceive cannot engage us. Thus, you must break or prevent patterns, except those created for strategic rhetorical effect. So: Vary your sentence lengths. In this passage, Reagan started with a six-word sentence. Then, a 13-word sentence. Then, a 12-word sentence, followed by a 28-word sentence.

Email Peter D. Andrei, the author of the Speak for Success collection and the President of Speak Truth Well LLC directly,

pandreibusiness@gmail.com

HOW TO AVOID INSTANTLY LOSING AUDIENCE ATTENTION

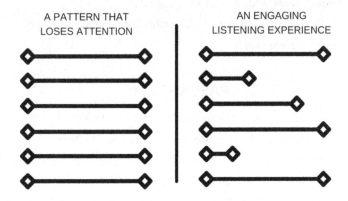

FIGURE 24: Varied sentence lengths produce intrigue and interest, creating an engaging and varied listening experience. Speaking sentences of the same length in sequence for an extended portion of your speech grows tremendously monotonous and loses attention. There is one caveat: it can be beneficial to periodically speak sentences of the same length when the meaning justifies it or when it achieves some rhetorical effect. However, in the absence of these conditions, stay away from same-length sentences. They bore people.

PASSAGE #25:

Above all, we must realize that no arsenal or no weapon in the arsenals of the world is so formidable as the will and moral courage of free men and women. It is a weapon our adversaries in today's world do not have. It is a weapon that we as Americans do have. Let that be understood by those who practice terrorism and prey upon their neighbors.

SECRET #54:

Stacked anaphora plus floating opposites.

"It is a weapon our adversaries in today's world do not have. It is a weapon that we as Americans do have."

Both sentences start with "It is a weapon…"

And the floating opposites are loose: they aren't as clear-cut as four words, with two contrasting adjectives modifying two contrasting nouns.

"It is a weapon our adversaries (item A) in today's world do not have (description A). It is a weapon that we as Americans (item B) do have (description B)."

Item A contrasts with item B, and description A with description B – an adaptation of the prototypical floating opposites form.

PASSAGE #26:

I'm told that tens of thousands of prayer meetings are being held on this day, and for that I'm deeply grateful. We are a nation under God, and I believe God intended for us to be free. It would be fitting and good, I think, if on each Inaugural Day in future years it should be declared a day of prayer.

SECRET #55:

The spectrum of the sacred and profane.

Every statement sits somewhere on a spectrum between sounding sacred and sounding profane.

Sacred is defined as "connected with God (or the gods) or dedicated to a religious purpose and so deserving veneration."

Profane is defined as "relating or devoted to that which is not sacred or biblical; secular rather than religious."

As you just saw in this passage, and as you probably saw in Clinton's inaugural address, evoking sacred moods and ideas with sacred emotional associations is extremely eloquent, even for the nonreligious. And evoking the sacred doesn't necessitate religious allusions or imagery.

You can make your subject appear sacred by speaking about it as if it were (and chances are, if you think deeply enough, it probably is). Talk about its stakes; what it means for people; what happens if it doesn't work out; why it appeals to things humans find inherently valuable and purposeful.

PASSAGE #27:

This is the first time in our history that this ceremony has been held, as you've been told, on this West Front of the Capitol. Standing here, one faces a magnificent vista, opening up on this city's special beauty and history. At the end of this open mall are those shrines to the giants on whose shoulders we stand.

SECRET #56:

Speak to the moment.

This is an extremely eloquent and captivating strategy. It's simple: Speak directly to something that's happening "right now, today, in this moment, as we speak…"

Connect the context of your immediate surroundings to your message in a way that advances your rhetorical objectives.

The Ancient Greek masters of rhetoric called this *Kairos*.

PASSAGE #28:

Directly in front of me, the monument to a monumental man, George Washington, father of our country. A man of humility who came to greatness reluctantly. He led America out of revolutionary victory into infant nationhood. Off to one side, the stately memorial to Thomas Jefferson. The Declaration of Independence flames with his eloquence. And then, beyond the Reflecting Pool, the dignified columns of the Lincoln Memorial. Whoever would understand in his heart the meaning of America will find it in the life of Abraham Lincoln.

SECRET #57:

"VSDC" verbs.

What's an "VSDC" verb? It's a visual verb that is specific, detail-oriented, and concrete. Reagan uses one here: "The Declaration of Independence *flames* with his eloquence."

It's even better if the VSDC verb is unusual and unique in the context of its use. Why? This acts as a subtle pattern-interrupt, breaking expectations and grabbing attention as a result.

Something that flames has a visual characteristic that is specific, detail-oriented, and concrete.

When you read that line, chances are you immediately pictured the Declaration of Independence enveloped in the hazy glow of fire. Chances are the sentence captivated your attention as a result.

PASSAGE #29:

Beyond those monuments to heroism is the Potomac River, and on the far shore the sloping hills of Arlington National Cemetery, with its row upon row of simple white markers bearing crosses or Stars of David. They add up to only a tiny fraction of the price that has been paid for our freedom.

SECRET #58:

Visually stimulating scenes.

The human mind engages with visually stimulating scenes. It's that simple. Our perception is predominantly visual. And describing visual scenes appeals to this, achieving immense eloquence.

In this passage, Reagan paints a full portrait of this scene. He invites listeners into it. He puts them there (if they weren't there already as listeners). And this controls attention with ease.

KEY INSIGHT:

One of the Most Magical Powers of Language is its Ability to Shape the Pictures We See in Our Mind's Eye.

Reagan Used This. Clinton Did Too. Painting Visual Scenes Directs a Drama on the Stages of the Audience's Minds.

This Drama Can Move Us to Hope and to Fear; to Aim and to Avoid; or in Reagan's Case, to Love, Respect, and Revere.

THE LITTLE-KNOWN POWER OF VISUAL LANGUAGE

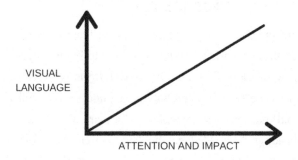

FIGURE 25: Humans are visual creatures. As the visual nature of language rises, so does the attention it receives and its persuasive impact.

PASSAGE #30:

Each one of those markers is a monument to the kind of hero I spoke of earlier. Their lives ended in places called Belleau Wood, The Argonne, Omaha Beach, Salerno, and halfway around the world on Guadalcanal, Tarawa, Pork Chop Hill, the Chosin Reservoir, and in a hundred rice paddies and jungles of a place called Vietnam.

SECRET #59:

"A1 4, and A2 4, and A3 1" pattern-interrupt construction.

This is a compelling pattern-interrupt construction.

Reagan lists "where their lives ended" (A1), and FOUR list items under this banner; places "halfway around the world" (A2), and FOUR list items under this banner; and in a place with "a hundred rice paddies and jungles" (A3) and ONE list item under this banner: Vietnam, which also happens to be looming closest in the national consciousness at this point.

See the structure of the pattern-interrupt? See how much more eloquent and engaging it is than a flat list?

PASSAGE #31:

Under one such marker lies a young man, Martin Treptow, who left his job in a small-town barbershop in 1917 to go to France with the famed Rainbow Division. There, on the western front, he was killed trying to carry a message between battalions under heavy artillery fire. We're told that on his body was found a diary. On the flyleaf under the heading, "My Pledge," he had written these words: "America must win this war. Therefore, I will work, I will save, I will sacrifice, I will endure, I will fight cheerfully and do my utmost, as if the issue of the whole struggle depended on me alone."

SECRET #60:

More attached adjectives.

Remember one of the critical functions of attached adjectives: Enumerating nuance. Illuminating aspects of a thing creating layered and engaging meaning.

We see this function on compelling and clear display in this passage: "Martin Treptow, who left his job in a *small-town* barbershop in 1917 to go to France with the *famed* Rainbow Division. There, on the western front, he was killed trying to carry a message between battalions under *heavy* artillery fire."

Small-town: There's something uniquely American about this subtle motif; it's the humble origins of a hero who came from little, not much; not from the opulence of New York, for example.

Famed: They're infamous; they're notorious for their devotion to duty; they're not a standard division.

Heavy: It's not a stray mortar shell here and there. It's persistent, rhythmic, deafening fire.

PASSAGE #32:

The crisis we are facing today does not require of us the kind of sacrifice that Martin Treptow and so many thousands of others were called upon to make. It does require, however, our best effort and our willingness to believe in ourselves and to believe in our capacity to perform great deeds, to believe that together with God's help we can and will resolve the problems which now confront us.

SECRET #61:

Micro-climax.

We talked about rhetorical climax – rapidly leaping from an idea to a more intensified idea, and then another, so on and so forth – and we discussed the jolt of intensity it can create.

Micro-climax delivers a similar jolt. Just the bite-sized version. And it happens in three words. Sometimes two, if you want.

Here's how Reagan used it: "...to believe that together with God's help we *can* and *will* resolve the problems which now confront us."

Get it? "Will" is more intense than "can."

The rapid jump produces a micro-rhetorical climax. And you can even do it in two words: "...we can- *will* resolve..."

PASSAGE #33:

And after all, why shouldn't we believe that? We are Americans. God bless you, and thank you.

...............................Chapter Summary...............................

- Reagan spoke with a distinct style: despite rhetorical similarities, Reagan and Clinton sound distinct.

- Reagan used sentence-level grammatical balance: his sentences have eloquent internal proportionality.
- Reagan used frequent reframing strategies, often layered over chiasmus, contrasts, and antitheticals.
- Reagan painted precise, specific, strategic, concrete visual imagery, presenting his message through visual scenes.
- Reagan spoke with a slightly less formal diction than Clinton, sounding more casual and relatable throughout.
- Reagan presented more narrative information about real events that occurred prior or during than Clinton did.

KEY INSIGHT:

No Rhetorical Device, Persuasive Strategy, or Eloquent Phrase Ought to Obscure Who You Are.

Your True Diction, Your True Persona, Your True Being... The Purpose of Rhetoric Is to Shape It, Not to Hide It.

YOUR RHETORICAL TOOLBOX (PART TWO)

1	Use Clinton's Rhetorical Secrets
1.1	Inclusive Pronouns Establish Empathy and Parity
1.2	Your Subject is What You're Talking About
1.3	Your Lens is the Perspective You Approach the Subject Through
1.4	Alliteration Starts Consecutive Words with the Same Sound
1.5	Alliterative Couples are Two Consecutive Alliterative Words
1.6	Fragmented Alliteration Has Intervening Words Breaking It Up
1.7	Reverse Alliteration Ends Words with the Same Sound
1.8	Tricolons are Lists of Three Creating Compelling Flow and Rhythm
1.9	Nested Rhetorical Devices Occur Within a Dominant Device
1.10	Opposing Structures, Meanings, Words, etc., Create Contrast
1.11	Matching Structures, Meanings, Words, etc., Create Symmetry
1.12	Superabundance is Rhetorical Addition; Expansion; Stretching
1.13	Intensifying Superabundance Adds a Pile of Intense Elaboration
1.14	"Verb-Saturated" Language Delivers Action-Oriented Narrative
1.15	Layered Devices Are of Equal Force and Occur Concurrently
1.16	In- and Out-Flow Occurs When One Word Ends Device A, Starts B
1.17	Fragmented Alliterative Couplets: "Strong and Stable."
1.18	Reverse Fragmented Alliteration: "Fight for What is Right."
1.19	Enumeratio Breaks Up an Item into its Constituent Parts

1.20	Assonance Repeats Vowel Sounds in Close Proximity
1.21	Consonance Repeats Consonant Sounds in Close Proximity
1.22	Parallelism Occurs When Segments Share Grammatical Structure
1.23	Loose Parallelism Occurs When Segments Only Share Grammar
1.24	Front-Back Alliteration: "Strong, Fast"
1.25	Phonetically Undone Couplet: Two Phonetics Undoing Each Other
1.26	Action-Oriented Language Creates a Self-Driven Narrative
1.27	Strict Parallelism is Identical Grammar and Some Word Repetition
1.28	Strictly Parallel Tricolon: Three Comma-Split Strict Parallels
1.29	Asyndeton Omits Grammatically Accurate Conjunctions
1.30	Pattern-Interrupts Break Away from a Preceding Pattern
1.31	Micro Devices Occur on Small Scales: Letters and Words
1.32	Macro Devices Occur on Large Scales: Paragraphs and Passages
1.33	X, X, YX Pattern-Interrupts: "From Time to Time... Our Time."
1.34	Simple Contrast: Two Contrasting Words in Close Proximity
1.35	Anaphora Starts Subsequent Sentences with the Same Words
1.36	Anaphora Paradigms are Anaphora-Based Structural Segments
1.37	Fragmented Anaphora Paradigms Have Intervening Material
1.38	X, YX Pattern-Interrupts: "It Can Be Done, and Done Fairly."
1.39	Stacked Pattern Interrupts Stack Pattern-Breaking Strategies

1.40	A, B1X, C1Y, D1Z Constructions: "For X, From X, To X"
1.41	Micro-Parallelism is Word or Segment-Level Parallelism
1.42	Stacked Micro-Parallelism Stacks Micro-Parallel Segments
1.43	Noun Couplets Emphasize an Item by Using Two Words for it
1.44	Stacked Contrasts Stack Contrasting Phrases Together
1.45	Symmetrical Word Choice Creates Rhetorical Unity
1.46	Inundating Contrasts Creates a "Superabundance" of Contrast
1.47	"While" Constructions Transition and Create Narrative Movement
1.48	Attached Adjectives Modify Directly Subsequent Nouns
1.49	Climax Arranges Items in Order of Increasing Intensity
1.50	Reverse Climax Arranges Items in Order of Decreasing Intensity
1.51	Letter-Level Flow: Rhetorical Symmetry at the Smallest Level
1.52	Tiered O-A Flow: A Particular Form of Letter-Level Flow
1.53	Themes Are Perspectives Through Which to View a Subject
1.54	Metaphors Equate Two Items
1.55	Theme-Indicating Metaphors Compare the Theme to Something
1.56	Rhetorical Emphasis Uses Components of Rhetoric to Emphasize
1.57	Periodic Sentences Place the Key Word in the Final Position
1.58	Stacked Periodic Segments Sequence Periodic Segments
1.59	Double Attached Adjectives: "America's Long Heroic Journey..."

1.60	A1, P1, P2, A2: "Let Us X with Y, with Z, and Let Us J"
1.61	Elevated and Figurative Language Uses Non-Pedestrian Words
2	**Use Reagan's Rhetorical Secrets**
2.1	Implicit Micro-Repetition: Word-Level Implied Repetition of a Word
2.2	Alliterative Attached Adjectives: "A Watching World…"
2.3	Example Triads Follow a Claim with Three Succinct Examples
2.4	Emotionally Triggering Words Create Visceral Reactions
2.5	Sententia Summarizes Preceding Material in a Hard-Hitting Way
2.6	Analogy: An Extended, Explanatory, Argumentative Similarity
2.7	Rhetorical Questions Pose Questions to the Audience
2.8	Frontloaded Transitions Capture Curiosity at a Segment's Start
2.9	N1, N1A, N1B, N1C, Y1: "not X by A, B, C, but X…"
2.10	Frames Are Established Relationships Between Things
2.11	Reframing Cleverly Shifts Around Preceding Frames
2.12	Second-Item Reversal Reframing: "X is A" Becomes "X is -A"
2.13	Breakaway Phrases Breach Patterns, Grabbing Attention
2.14	Explicit Chiasmus: Words, Constructions, or Concepts Reversed
2.15	Implicit Chiasmus: Reversed Portion of Chiasmus is Implied
2.16	Antitheticals: "Not X, But Y"
2.17	Reversed Antitheticals: "X, Not Y"

2.18	Stacked Reverse Antitheticals: "X, Not Y, Not Z"
2.19	Sentence-Intervened Repetition: "The Price… Pay that Price"
2.20	NA1, YA2 Constructions: "Not A if 1… A if 2"
2.21	Conduplicatio Repeats a Word Across Segments, Sentences, etc.
2.22	A1, A2, A3, B1, B2, B3: "Our X, Our Y, Our Z; the X, the Y, the Z"
2.23	Anadiplosis: The Last Word of a Segment as the First of the Next
2.24	Loose Anadiplosis: Roughly the Last Word Repeated Roughly First
2.25	Enveloped Phonetic Repetition: "Our Country… Our Countrymen"
2.26	Hypophora: Asking and then Answering a Rhetorical Question
2.27	Open Loops Are Created by Triggered but Unanswered Curiosity
2.28	Hypophora-Based Open Loops Create the Loop with Hypophora
2.29	Borrowed Eloquence Uses Relevant, Eloquent Quotations
2.30	Personal Style is the Unique Aspects of an Individual's Language
2.31	Universal Themes Crop Up Over and Over Despite Personal Styles
2.32	Varied Sentence Lengths Create Intrigue and Maintain Attention
2.33	Stacked Anaphora Sequences Anaphora Paradigms
2.34	Floating Opposites: "Adjective A Noun B, Adjective -A Noun -B"
2.35	Sacred-Profane Spectrum: Everyday to Sanctified Language
2.36	Speaking to the Moment: Stating What is Happening "Now"
2.37	"VSDC" Verbs: Visual, Specific, Detail-Oriented, Concrete Verbs

2.38	Visually Stimulating Scenes Draw Listeners into a Mental Movie
2.39	A14, A24, A31: "A1 (1, 2, 3, 4), A2 (1, 2, 3, 4), A3 (1)"
2.40	Micro-Climax: Word-Level Rhetorical Climax
3	**Use JFK's Rhetorical Secrets**

Email Peter D. Andrei, the author of the Speak for Success
collection and the President of Speak Truth Well LLC directly.

pandreibusiness@gmail.com

KEY INSIGHT:

A Picture is Worth a Thousand
Words. But Words Can Paint a
Thousand Pictures.

As You Speak, Your Audience
Will See Things in The Theater
of Their Imaginations. What
Will You Show Them?

REAGAN'S VISUALLY STIMULATING SCENES

I

West Front of the Capital
Magnificent vista
City's special beauty and history
Open mall

II

Shrines
Monument to George Washington
Memorial of Thomas Jefferson
The Reflecting Pool
Lincoln Memorial

III

Potomac River
Far shore
Sloping hills
Arlington National Cemetery
Simple white markers

IV

Belleau Wood, Argonne, Omaha Beach....
Halfway around the world
Guadalcanal, Tarawa, Pork Chop Hill...
Jungles of a place called Vietnam....

AN EXPANSIVE VERBAL-VISUAL JOURNEY
AROUND THE GLOBE, STARTING "HERE" ON THE
"WEST FRONT" AND ENDING IN "VIETNAM"

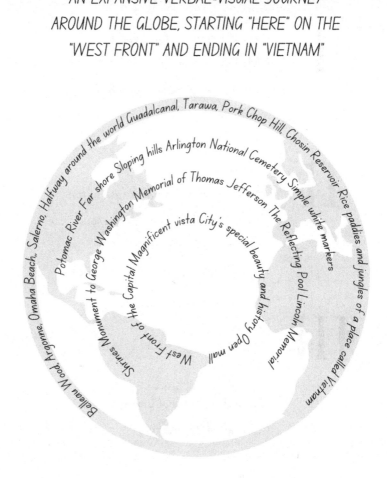

FIRST, THE IMMEDIATE SURROUNDINGS.
SECOND, FURTHER MONUMENTS.
THIRD, FURTHER MONUMENTS... OF WAR.
FOURTH, WARZONES OF THE PAST AND PRESENT.

Claim These Free Resources that Will Help You Unleash the Power of Your Words and Speak with Confidence. Visit www.speakforsuccesshub.com/toolkit for Access.

18 Free PDF Resources

12 Iron Rules for Captivating Story, 21 Speeches that Changed the World, 341-Point Influence Checklist, 143 Persuasive Cognitive Biases, 17 Ways to Think On Your Feet, 18 Lies About Speaking Well, 137 Deadly Logical Fallacies, 12 Iron Rules For Captivating Slides, 371 Words that Persuade, 63 Truths of Speaking Well, 27 Laws of Empathy, 21 Secrets of Legendary Speeches, 19 Scripts that Persuade, 12 Iron Rules For Captivating Speech, 33 Laws of Charisma, 11 Influence Formulas, 219-Point Speech-Writing Checklist, 21 Eloquence Formulas

Claim These Free Resources that Will Help You Unleash the Power of Your Words and Speak with Confidence. Visit <u>www.speakforsuccesshub.com/toolkit</u> for Access.

30 Free Video Lessons

We'll send you one free video lesson every day for 30 days, written and recorded by Peter D. Andrei. Days 1-10 cover authenticity, the prerequisite to confidence and persuasive power. Days 11-20 cover building self-belief and defeating communication anxiety. Days 21-30 cover how to speak with impact and influence, ensuring your words change minds instead of falling flat. Authenticity, self-belief, and impact – this course helps you master three components of confidence, turning even the most high-stakes presentations from obstacles into opportunities.

Claim These Free Resources that Will Help You Unleash the Power of Your Words and Speak with Confidence. Visit www.speakforsuccesshub.com/toolkit for Access.

2 Free Workbooks

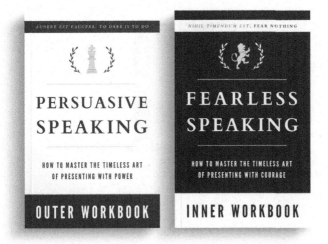

We'll send you two free workbooks, including long-lost excerpts by Dale Carnegie, the mega-bestselling author of *How to Win Friends and Influence People* (5,000,000 copies sold). *Fearless Speaking* guides you in the proven principles of mastering your inner game as a speaker. *Persuasive Speaking* guides you in the time-tested tactics of mastering your outer game by maximizing the power of your words. All of these resources complement the Speak for Success collection.

SPEAK FOR SUCCESS COLLECTION BOOK

II

ELOQUENCE CHAPTER

IV

THE THIRD SPEECH:

John F. Kennedy's Inaugural Address

"AN END, AS WELL AS A BEGINNING..."

J FK DELIVERED THIS ADDRESS on January 20, 1961. He wrote and spoke these words when he assumed leadership of the world's most powerful nation as humanity teetered on the knife-edge of engulfing the world in a nuclear inferno – destroying, in the span of days, what millions and billions of men and women bled, wept, and died to build. Do you think he would wing it? Let's find out. While parts one and two focused on passage-level analysis, this part, part three, also pays due to rhetorical devices and strategies that occur across passages, presenting the rhetorical continuity responsible for producing such unparalleled, unforgettable, unbeatable eloquence. Let us begin.

PASSAGE #1:

Vice President Johnson, Mr. Speaker, Mr. Chief Justice, President Eisenhower, Vice President Nixon, President Truman, reverend clergy, fellow citizens, we observe today not a victory of party, but a celebration of freedom – symbolizing an end, as well as a beginning – signifying renewal, as well as change. For I have sworn before you and Almighty God the same solemn oath our forebears prescribed nearly a century and three quarters ago.

SECRET #62:

Inclusive greetings, antithesis layered over paradox layered under grammatical parallelism, strategic, connotation, alliterative couplets.

JFK begins with honorary greetings. He thanks a few key, important people. But as JFK always does, he also acknowledges the common man and woman.

Here's how: by saying "fellow citizens."

Why? Because this way, everyone feels acknowledged. Nobody feels neglected. Everyone feels noticed.

Then, he immediately uses an inclusive pronoun.

One of JFK's most common rhetorical devices is antithesis. Not only in his inaugural address, but in all of his speeches. JFK seems to love things like contrast, paradox, antithesis, apposition, floating opposites, etc. This is exactly what makes his speech so captivating.

Here's how he used antithesis: "not a victory of party, but a celebration of freedom." It forces the audience to make a mental assumption of what comes next, and then satisfies or denies it. It makes the audience think "if it's not X, what is it? Maybe Y." Then the speech either confirms or denies their assumption.

In the same antithetical sentence, he uses paradox: "symbolizing an end, as well as a beginning – signifying renewal, as well as change." And he doesn't stop there: he ends with a paradox justification. He refers to the history of presidential inaugurations, and presents himself as just another man in a series of men before him. This presents humility, but also hope for improvement.

He's saying "I'm part of a miraculous process of democratic freedom that is much bigger than me, but I also will bring new offerings to the table."

But there's even more rhetorical artistry to this: he uses parallelism, when he says "symbolizing (verb) an end (noun), as well as (adverbial phrase) a beginning (noun) – signifying (verb) renewal (noun), as well as (adverbial phrase) change (change)."

The two phrases are grammatically parallel: (verbing) (a noun) (adverbial phrase) (a contrasting noun); (verbing) (a noun) (adverbial phrase) (a contrasting noun).

But what does parallelism do? It creates grammatical and rhythmic symmetry, which emphasizes contrasts. Nested in this parallelism are contrasting nouns. "Ending" versus "beginning." "Renewal" (bringing back something old) versus "change" (starting something new). The verbs are symmetrical and alliterative: "signifying (...) symbolizing." The adverbs are symmetrical: "as well as (...) as well as." The grammatical structure is symmetrical. But the nouns contrast, and all this symmetry advertises the contrasts. The contrasts contrast with each other, but they also contrast with the symmetry surrounding them.

JFK also uses alliterative couplets: "*s*ame *s*olemn." And he uses consecutive (or stacked) alliterative couplets too: "*s*ame *s*olemn *o*ath *o*ur."

Further, JFK sprinkles elevated, connotative, and evocative language throughout the speech. Elevated language refers to sophisticated but simple language (almost all of the following examples are so I won't enumerate this). Connotative language describes words that carry an extra nuance of meaning. Evocative language refers to words with emotional implications.

Some examples? "Fellow citizens" is connotative: fellow implies brotherhood, parity, and relation.

"Victory" is connotative: victory implies a divided political climate where one side competes against the other.

"Celebration" is evocative: celebration carries many emotional implications of positive sentiment; of achievement, and satisfaction.

"Freedom" is evocative: freedom evokes American values near and dear to everyone in his audience. (And probably everyone everywhere – who doesn't like freedom?)

"Signifying" is connotative: signifying implies significance. Compare that to a similar but un-connotative verb, like "showing." The impact is drastically different.

"Renewal" is evocative: it evokes the emotion of rejuvenation, and connotes that old elements will remain if they are valuable.

"Sworn" is connotative: it adds a layer of importance. Compare that to a soft, un-connotative word: "agreed."

"Almighty" is evocative: it evokes the emotion of deference, respect, and awe.

Think we're done with passage one? Just about.

Some more hidden techniques remain.

JFK uses delayed transitions. This is starting sentences with words like "for, and, so, but," and the like: fast, one-word transitions which string along audience attention by connecting the previous sentence to the current sentence with as little as two letters.

JFK could have said "175 years ago," but instead he chose "nearly a century and three quarters ago."

It's a small stylistic choice, but which one sounds better? More dramatic? More meaningful? More significant? More eloquent?

The second form is also longer, which makes sense considering that he wants to emphasize the sheer length of intervening time.

"Symbolizing an end, as well as a beginning – signifying renewal, as well as change," is also Chiasmus.

PASSAGE #2:

The world is very different now. For man holds in his mortal hands the power to abolish all forms of human poverty and all forms of human life. And yet the same revolutionary beliefs for which our forebears fought are still at issue around the globe - the belief that the rights of man come not from the generosity of the state, but from the hand of God.

SECRET #63:

Then-and-now constructions, delayed transitions, crescendo sentences, structure-meaning alignment, metaphor and figurative language, fragmented alliteration, standard alliteration, enveloped phonetic repetition, and assonance, layered.

The very first sentence completes the second part of a two-part structure. It's called the then-and-now: In the previous passage, he presents a "then." He says "For I have sworn before you and Almighty God the same solemn oath our forebears prescribed nearly a century and three quarters ago." And in the start of this passage, he completes it with the "now" when he says "The world is very different now."

THE LITTLE-KNOWN POWER OF CONTRASTING LANGUAGE

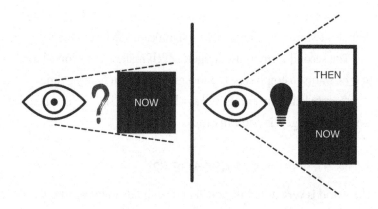

FIGURE 26: The then and now strategy produces contrast by comparing the past to the present. By judiciously shaping the set of contextual items available to listeners, the "then" step shapes the perception of the target item: the "now" step. This moment makes sense in the context of the past, and selecting that context deliberately shapes the perception of the current moment however you see fit.

JFK also uses a delayed transition to transition to the second sentence: "For..." But then he doubles up on delayed transitions. Delayed transitions are crisp, clear, commanding transitions that slide audience attention from one sentence to the next. And he uses a double delayed transition to move from sentences two to three: "And (delayed transition one) yet (delayed transition two)..."

Delayed transitions carry high word economy: they transmit a large amount of meaning with a small number of words. As such, they lower cognitive load and grab attention.

JFK also uses a crescendo sentence pattern. The length of the sentences grows throughout this passage. And it causes increased intensity, and a sense of climax.

Sentence one: 6 words. Crisp, clear, commanding.

Sentence two: 22 words. A longer, more intense sentence.

Sentence three: 39 words. A long, flowing, winding sentence that explodes with intensity and crashes onto itself like a wave.

Throughout this speech, JFK mirrors the meaning of his words with supporting rhetorical components: Not only does he use a crescendo sentence pattern in which each sentence becomes longer and more grammatically complex than the last, but he also speaks words in each of those sentences that are more intense than the last.

See how he uses structure-meaning alignment? See how he uses rhetorical devices and components that mirror his words? Masterful.

Moving on. You know about JFK's paradoxical contrast obsession, right? We see some more: "For man holds in his mortal hands the power to abolish all forms of human poverty and all forms of human life."

He also uses more attached adjectives. "The world is very different now. For man holds in his *mortal* hands the power to abolish all forms of human poverty and all forms of human life. And yet the same *revolutionary* beliefs for which our forebears fought are still at issue around the globe – the belief that the rights of man come not from the generosity of the state, but from the hand of God."

"Hands" versus "mortal hands."

"Beliefs" versus "revolutionary beliefs."

See how that makes it so much more meaningful? The fact that the hands which can "abolish all forms of human poverty and all forms of human life" are mortal hands makes it so much more meaningful. It emphasizes that this godlike power is still held by mortal, flawed, passing hands.

And think about the fact that the beliefs aren't just ordinary beliefs, but revolutionary ones. Simply by moving through the passage and attaching adjectives to nouns, JFK consistently adds nuance to his message.

Some more classic antithesis: "Not from the generosity of the state, but from the hand of God."

"Not from X, but from Y."

We already talked about this, it's just another example.

And JFK avoided a mistake when he said "the generosity of the state" instead of the "state's generosity." Why? Because that audibly sounds the same as "states." On paper, you can clearly see it: "state's" versus "states." But in speech you can't distinguish it. They sound the same but one of them is a grammatical mistake. And the form "(possession) of the state" prevents this.

Further, he consistently uses metaphor and figurative language. Can man truly hold an ability in his hands? No. And layered under metaphorical and figurative language is the use of religious motifs: "...from the hand of God." And this also ties to his reference of mortal, human hands, which he says have godlike power. At the beginning of the paragraph, he mentions the mortal human hands holding godlike power, and at the end, he mentions the actual hand of God. Coincidence? I think not.

And this passage is filled with connotative, elevated, and evocative language: "For man holds in his *mortal* hands the *power* to *abolish* all forms of *human poverty* and all forms of *human life*. And yet the same *revolutionary* beliefs for which our *forebears fought* are still at issue around the *globe* – the belief that the *rights of man* come not from the *generosity* of the *state*, but from *the hand of God.*"

Finally, take a look at this phrase: "for which our forebears fought." Fragmented and standard alliteration: "*f*or which our *for*ebears *f*ought." Enveloped phonetic repetition: "*for* which our *for*ebears fought." Assonance: "f*or* which *our* f*or*ebears f*ou*ght."

KEY INSIGHT:

Assonance Creates an Alluring Flow, Like a Soft Song. Consonance Creates a Strong Rhythm, Like a War Drum.

Together, They Create an Auditory Masterpiece.

PASSAGE #3:

We dare not forget today that we are the heirs of that first revolution. Let the word go forth from this time and place, to friend and foe alike, that the torch has been passed to a new generation of Americans – born in this century, tempered by war, disciplined by a hard and bitter peace, proud of our ancient heritage – and unwilling to witness or permit the slow undoing of those human rights to which this Nation has always been committed, and to which we are committed today at home and around the world.

SECRET #64:

Enumeratio, auxiliary words versus meaningful words, reducing auxiliary words, bundling auxiliary words, bundling meaningful words, emphasizing meaning with placement and rhetoric, formal versus pedestrian auxiliaries.

This passage is dominated by one rhetorical device in particular: enumeratio. He enumerates multiple aspects of "a new generation of Americans," namely that they are "born in this century, tempered by war, disciplined by a hard and bitter peace, proud of our ancient heritage."

Instead of saying "a new generation of Americans," and leaving it there, JFK breaks it down persuasively and eloquently.

He also uses inclusive pronouns that command his audience as a leader. He says "we dare not forget today that we are the heirs of that first revolution." This is how a leader of JFK's caliber should talk: He sets goals for a "we," including himself. He sets goals for his team. He doesn't set goals for his followers. He doesn't say "you shall," but "we shall." In this way he both commands and expresses humility and a sense of purpose.

Now: Any time we see a speaker like JFK repeat words, we must ask ourselves why. Answering this question will yield tremendous insights into the hidden machinery of JFK's speech writing team, the subconscious and subtextual messages JFK sought to impart, and the set of definitive buzzwords that embody his theme.

We see these words repeated: "Revolution, human, rights, committed, world / globe, new."

Yes: He repeats words like "the, or, for," and the like more. But that is meaningless. Repeating unusual, infrequent words signifies deliberate, intentional repetition for a specific purpose. So, what's JFK's big message? What's the whole idea he's illustrating in this passage? "That this new revolution is committed to preserving human rights around the globe."

This brings us to a discussion of auxiliary words and meaningful words. Auxiliary words simply connect the meaningful words together. Alone, they have no concrete meaning. Let's try to analyze this segment. I'll mark auxiliary words with an A, and meaningful words with an M. "...unwilling (m) to (a) witness (m) or (a) permit (m) the (a) slow (m) undoing (m) of (a) those (a) human (m) rights (m) to (a) which (a) this (a) Nation (m) has (a) always (m) been (m) committed (m), and (a) to (a) which (a) we (a) are (a) committed (m) today (m) at (a) home (m) and (a) around (m) the (a) world (m)."

Good speech lessens the number of auxiliary words. This doesn't mean to get rid of all auxiliary words. That's grammatical nonsense. Auxiliary words are absolutely necessary for supporting the meaningful words. Without the auxiliary words, the meaningful words lose meaning. They become nonsense.

So, let me be more specific: Good speech is cutting unnecessary auxiliary words, bundling auxiliary words together, bundling meaningful words together, and using placement and rhetorical devices to emphasize meaningful words.

Sentences should begin and end with meaningful words, which should occur consecutively in packets. And, in order to avoid diluting those packets of punchy, meaningful words, you should also bundle the intervening auxiliary words together.

So, a good segment (or set of words between grammatical separators) would be this: (separator) m m m a a a m m m (separator) (By grammatical separators, I mean periods, commas, or anything else that breaks apart long phrases into units, which would usually be signaled by a pause in speech).

As we can see, JFK mostly follows this rule. He starts and ends sentences or grammatical sub-structures with meaningful words, and connects them with strings of auxiliary words whenever possible: (meaning one) (connection) (meaning two) equals (new meaning).

This is the optimal grammatical pattern for emphasizing meaningful words and reducing the amount of audience attention wasted on auxiliary words.

Auxiliary words are often combined into contractions. "That (a) is (a)" becomes "that's (a)." This limits the number of auxiliary words, but it ruins the air of purpose and formality JFK wanted to create. So, he uses almost no contractions.

Now, let's talk about the auxiliary words he chooses to use. Instead of saying "should" and "because," which are everyday pedestrian phrases, he replaces them with the more formal and purposeful "shall" and "for." And these are just two examples of JFK replacing pedestrian auxiliary phrases with elevated ones.

You're probably questioning me on this.

"Did JFK really pay so much attention to his auxiliary phrases?"

"Does it really make a difference?"

"Does he really bundle together auxiliary phrases so that he can end phrases with meaningful words?"

Yes, yes, and yes.

For example, he said "...and unwilling to witness or permit the slow undoing of those human rights to (a) which (a) (bundled auxiliary words) this Nation has always been committed (m) (the periodic position emphasizes the meaningful words)."

He could have said "and unwilling to witness or permit the slow undoing of those human rights which (a) (un-bundled auxiliary word) this Nation has always been committed (m) to (a) (auxiliary word in a place a meaningful word belongs for emphasis)."

But no. He did the right thing, and bundled the auxiliary words "which" and "to" together, so that he could end with the evocative, elevated, connotative word "committed." And in doing so, he emphasized that sense of "commitment," instead of wasting the most precious part of the sentence on the word "to."

HOW AUXILIARIES CAN HELP NOT HURT YOUR MESSAGE

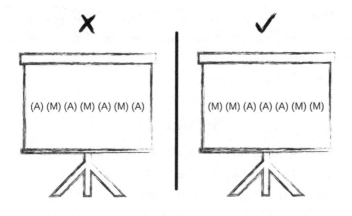

FIGURE 27: This exemplifies the four auxiliary algorithms. First, remove unnecessary auxiliaries. Second, bundle meaningful words. Third, bundle auxiliary words. Fourth, place meaningful words in positions of inherent emphasis.

KEY INSIGHT:

Put the Important Stuff in the Important Places, and Put the Rest Wherever is Left Over.

Don't Let the Crucial Ideas Languish in Obscurity. They Deserve the Linguistic Spotlight.

PASSAGE #4:

Let every nation know, whether it wishes us well or ill, that we shall pay any price, bear any burden, meet any hardship, support any friend, oppose any foe, in order to assure the survival and the success of liberty. This much we pledge – and more.

SECRET #65:

Alliteration-based in-flow and out-flow, micro-parallelism, rising and falling sentence lengths, dual contrasts, three short-long versus two long-short, meta-contrasts.

In this passage, fragmented alliteration flows into reverse alliteration which flows back into more fragmented alliteration which breaks and then goes back into fragmented alliteration.

"Let every nation know, whether it wishes us well (fragmented alliteration ends, fragmented reverse alliteration begins) or ill, that we shall (fragmented reverse alliteration ends, fragmented alliteration begins) pay any price, bear any burden, (all alliterative phrases break) meet any hardship, support any friend, oppose any foe, in order to assure the (short fragmented alliteration) survival and the success of liberty. This much we pledge – and more."

The end of the first fragmented alliteration is the start of the reverse alliteration. The word that ends the fragmented alliteration (*w*ell) starts the reverse alliteration (we*ll*). The word well both ends the fragmented alliteration and starts the fragmented reverse alliteration.

So, these two forms of alliteration overlap on the word *well*. These overlapped forms of fragmented alliteration create rhythm, captivating flow, and eloquent, memorable, poetic speech.

Right at the end of the reverse alliteration begins the next fragmented alliteration: "*p*ay any *p*rice," "*b*ear any *b*urden." The passage ends with a short use of fragmented alliteration: "the *s*uccess and the *s*urvival of liberty."

This phrase is also an example of micro-parallelism nested within the alliteration (or more accurately, alliteration nested within micro parallelism). JFK could have said "the success and survival of liberty." In fact, that would have been grammatically expedient. But he wanted to create micro-parallelism. He wanted what came before the "and" to mirror what came after the "and," creating the construction "(phrase one) and (phrase two)," where phrase one and phrase two are grammatically symmetrical.

Are "the success" and "survival" grammatically symmetrical? No. Are "the success" and "the survival" grammatically symmetrical? Yes, in the form "(article) (noun)." Does this seem insignificant? It's not: this micro-parallelism contributes to the polished sense of the speech.

JFK also uses anaphora. He opens the anaphora paradigm in this passage. In the last passage, he started a segment with: "Let the word go forth..." And now he begins with: "Let every nation know."

But these two openings are also grammatically parallel. They are loosely parallel: "Let (verb) the word (noun) go (verb) forth (adverb)..." and "Let (verb) every (adjective) nation (noun) know (verb)..." It's loose parallelism in the form "Let a noun verb."

But let's revisit the main part of this section. One particular rhetorical device dominates it. The others nest within this dominant device.

"Let every nation know, whether it wishes us well or ill, that we shall pay any price (micro-parallel phrase one), bear any burden (micro-parallel phrase two), meet any hardship (micro-parallel phrase three), support any friend (micro-parallel phrase four), oppose any foe (micro-parallel phrase five), in order to assure the survival and the success of liberty. This much we pledge – and more."

Pay any price (verb any noun). Bear any burden (verb any noun). Meet any hardship (verb any noun). Support any friend (verb any noun). Oppose any foe (verb any noun).

And as you can see by the length (simply by looking at where the lines end on the page), these segments crest in length like a wave; they rise, then they fall.

Pay any price.

Bear any burden.

Meet any hardship.

Support any friend.

Oppose any foe.

THE ELOQUENCE OF THE CRESCENDO SENTENCE PATTERN

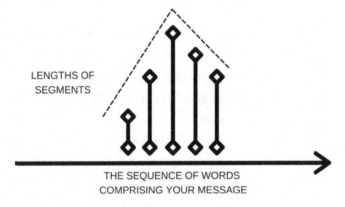

FIGURE 28: The lengths of the segments in this portion of the passage rise and fall like a wave, creating a captivating cadence and an engaging rhythm.

JFK loves nesting rhetorical devices, overlapping rhetorical devices, and sequencing rhetorical devices. He always has one "active" device, if not more. These basic bastions of eloquence render JFK's speech timeless and beautiful.

But let's return to those micro-parallel phrases. There is more to discuss. "Pay any price" is alliterative, with the verb shorter than the noun. "Bear any burden" is also alliterative, again with the verb shorter than the noun. "Meet any hardship" breaks the alliteration, but the rhythm of a short verb and a long noun continues. "Support any friend" reverses the rhythm from a short verb and a long noun to a long verb and a short noun. "Oppose any foe" continues the rhythm of a long verb and a short noun.

Let's zoom in on those final two: "support any friend" and "oppose any foe." They are not only rhythmically symmetrical and grammatically parallel: they are dual contrasts. The previous three items (paying prices, bearing burdens, and meeting hardships) echo the same sentiment, phrased in the same way: with a long verb and a short noun. These two contrasts break from the previous three by the act of contrasting itself (supporting versus opposing, friend versus foe). But they also reverse the long verb short noun paradigm. These subtle twists, turns, deliberate arrangements and careful proportionalities add up. They emphasize and empower. This embodies JFK's method of always using at least one active rhetorical device, and flowing multiple devices in and out of each other.

There are three more notable lessons here. The repetition of "any" solidifies the parallelism and emphasizes America's strength, versatility, and flexibility. The repeated action verbs "pay, bear, meet, support, oppose," build rhythm and grab audience attention. The use of "in order to" instead of "because" elevates JFK's speech by opting for elevated auxiliaries instead of common-place ones.

PASSAGE #5:

To those old allies whose cultural and spiritual origins we share, we pledge the loyalty of faithful friends. United, there is little we cannot do in a host of cooperative ventures. Divided, there is little we can do – for we dare not meet a powerful challenge at odds and split asunder.

SECRET #66:

Passage-level anaphora paradigms, comma symmetry, alliteration micro, fragmented, and reversed, the attached adjective algorithm, loose parallelism nesting contrasts.

You don't know this now, but this passage begins a second anaphora paradigm that dominates the remainder of this speech.

This closes the "let noun verb" anaphora paradigm and opens up a completely new one. You'll see what I mean in the next five passages.

HOW ANAPHORA PARADIGMS STRUCTURE A MESSAGE

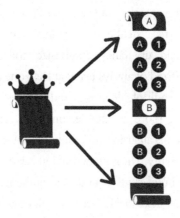

FIGURE 29: Anaphora paradigms accentuate the segmented structure of a speech by applying a different anaphora paradigm for each of the segments.

JFK also uses comma symmetry, a form of micro-parallelism that mirrors what comes before the comma with what comes after. Here's when: "(...) we share, we pledge (...)." This is nothing more than micro-parallelism mirrored across a comma.

We see micro-fragmented-reverse alliteration when he says "cultural and spiritual origins."

"Micro-fragmented-reverse alliteration? Sounds like a stretch." I assume that's what you're thinking. But let me ask you this: Do you think a new president in what is arguably the most critical moment of American history, who is writing his inaugural address, doesn't break it down to this level? And think about his army of speech writers. Don't you think they painstakingly analyze every word, deciding whether they could replace it with something better? They absolutely do.

There are three parts to this. It is micro because it occurs at the level of two words. It is fragmented because the word "and" separates the two alliterative words. It is reverse alliteration because it rhymes in the traditional sense (cul*tural* and spiri*tual*).

It is no coincidence that the army of speech writers wrote "cultural and spiritual" instead of "cultural" and something else, or something else and "spiritual." When a speaker of this importance is giving a speech of this importance, every word is chosen for a specific purpose. Every single word has a deliberate, intentional impact, both aesthetically and meaningfully. Some other possibilities would have been cultural and divine; cultural and sacred; civic and spiritual.

Now, if you're looking for non-micro-non-reversed-non-fragmented alliteration, just plain alliteration, he uses that too, in the same sentence (at the end): "(...) faithful friends."

He also uses more contrasting phrases, enveloping floating opposites in parallel sentences: "United, there is little we cannot do... Divided, there is little we can do..." While parallelism refers to the identical grammatical structures, I define identical words in identical positions as strict parallelism and purely grammatical symmetries as "loose parallelism."

Further, JFK used countless emphatic attached adjectives. I imagine the process is something like this: He writes down what he means to say without adjectives. He scans through looking for nouns and verbs in need of rhetorical elaboration. He inserts an attached adjective right before the noun or verb to strategically emphasize a particular quality of the item.

Step one: "To those allies whose origins we share, we pledge the loyalty of friends. United, there is little we cannot do in a host of ventures. Divided, there is little we can do – for we dare not meet a challenge and split."

Step two: "To those *allies* whose *origins* we share, we pledge the loyalty of *friends*. United, there is little we cannot do in a host of *ventures*. Divided, there is little we can do – for we dare not *meet* a *challenge* and split asunder."

Step three: "To those old allies whose cultural and spiritual origins we share, we pledge the loyalty of faithful friends. United, there is little we cannot do in a host of cooperative ventures. Divided, there is little we can do – for we dare not meet a powerful challenge at odds and split asunder."

Each of these adjectives fulfills a specific purpose, emphasizing or implying a specific quality and adding a strategic layer of meaning.

Compare allies with old allies. The attached adjective emphasizes the strength, reliability, and value of the bond. Why? Because old alliances are more likely to be stronger, more reliable, and more valuable than new and tenuous ones.

Compare origins with cultural and spiritual origins. The attached adjective emphasizes the depth and nuance of the shared origins. It emphasizes the two-fold common roots, found in their culture and spirit. This kind of similarity inspires allegiances that endure.

Compare friends with faithful friends. The attached adjective emphasizes the reliability and strength of the bond, once again. This is exactly what JFK would want to do to maximize his persuasive impact.

Compare ventures with cooperative ventures. The attached adjective emphasizes that for international and global ventures, instead of going at them alone, the old allies with shared cultural and spiritual origins (that are also faithful friends) should cooperate.

Compare challenge with powerful challenge. The attached adjective emphasizes the magnitude of the challenge, which acts as justification for the need for faithful friends who share cultural and spiritual origins to work together on the cooperative venture.

Simply by adding these strategic, emphatic attached adjectives, JFK communicated more meaning with more strategic emphasis, rhetorical force, and persuasive power.

WHY ATTACHED ADJECTIVES EASILY INFLUENCE PEOPLE

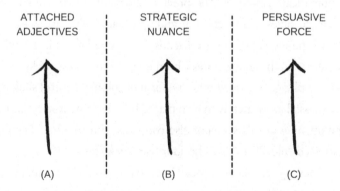

FIGURE 30: As you add attached adjectives, the strategic nuance enclosed therein rises, which increases the overall persuasive force of the message.

PASSAGE #6:

To those new states whom we welcome to the ranks of the free, we pledge our word that one form of colonial control shall not have passed away merely to be replaced by a far more iron tyranny. We shall not always expect to find them supporting our view. But we shall always hope to find them strongly supporting their own freedom – and to remember that, in the past, those who foolishly sought power by riding the back of the tiger ended up inside.

SECRET #67:

Unity through anaphora, periodic sentences, thematic unity through repetition, contrasted periodic words with phonetic "echo," templatization, contrasting words with positional symmetry.

The opening of this segment uses anaphora and loose grammatical symmetry. The previous segment began like so: "To those old allies whose cultural and spiritual origins we share, we pledge the loyalty of faithful friends." This one begins in a similar manner: "To those new states whom we welcome to the ranks of the free, we pledge our word that one form of colonial control shall not have passed away merely to be replaced by a far more iron tyranny." The opening of this segment also contrasts with the first. Then he addressed "old allies." Now he addresses "new states."

Opening consecutive segments with parallel or anaphoric sentences unites those segments, mirroring their categorization of meaning in the structure of the speech with rhetorical constructions.

There's more layered over this passage.

Alliteration: "whom we welcome."

Alliterative couplets: "colonial control," "strongly supporting."

Periodic sentences "ranks of the *free*, (...) iron *tyranny.*"

Repetition of words to create unifying themes: "new, pledge, free / freedom, support, power," etc.

Inclusive pronouns: repetition of "we."

Elevated, evocative, and connotative word choice.

Non-pedestrian auxiliary words: "shall," not "should."

Positive and hopeful language.

Contrast: "ranks of the free, (...) iron tyranny." The endings of the two periodic words seem to echo each other phonetically; when you hear the tyrannee, the "ee" of free still resounds in your mind, echoing over the sentence and creating a sort of implicit rhyme. The periodic position of free empowers this effect. Words in periodic positions tend to stick in the mind longer.

HOW TO USE THE POSITIONS OF INHERENT EMPHASIS

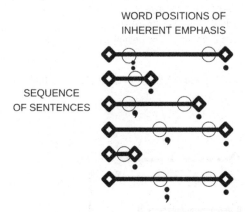

FIGURE 31: The word positions of inherent emphasis in the sequence of sentences are circled. Note that the first word is also a position of inherent emphasis.

THE RELATIONSHIP BETWEEN EMPHASIS AND MEMORY

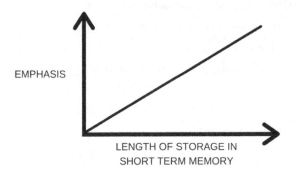

FIGURE 32: As the emphasis placed on a statement, word, sentence, segment, paragraph, idea, concept, or unit of meaning rises, so does the length of that item's stay in the short-term memory of the audience. Emphasis is, of course, achievable in multiple ways: while we are currently focusing on positional emphasis, there are many modes of emphasis, like vocal emphasis and gesture emphasis.

HOW EMPHASIS PRODUCES RHETORICAL "ECHO"

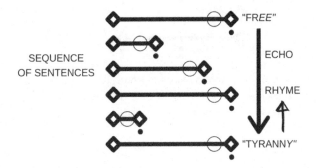

FIGURE 33: Emphasis increases the stay of a word in the short-term memory of the audience. Because the word "free" was placed in a position of inherent emphasis, it

stayed in short-term memory banks, allowing it to "resound" over the sentence and "echo" with "tyranny," many words further in the speech.

There are three new elements for analysis here. First, templatization: a repeated pattern; the same pattern with a different subject; repetitive structural organization. Second, contrasting ending phrases in periodic sentences. Third, unique metaphor.

Let's start with templatization. It's an incredibly powerful and versatile speech writing tool. Templatization refers to repetitive word templates that form a pattern. To write more content, you simply insert new subjects into the framework of an old template. This is the second time JFK uses this template: "To those (insert group) who (insert relationship to the 'we'), we pledge (insert pledge)." This was the first time: "To those old allies whose cultural and spiritual origins we share, we pledge the loyalty of faithful friends." This is the second time: "To those new states whom we welcome to the ranks of the free, we pledge our word that one form of colonial control shall not have passed away merely to be replaced by a far more iron tyranny."

This builds rhythm, creates memorable turns of phrase, makes speech-writing easier, simplifies the brainstorming process, and captivates the audience, all while emphasizing the meta-message (at this point, it is "saying X to Y") which raises comprehension. Further, it subtly expresses unity and how each portion of the speech relates to the whole.

What about contrasting phrases in periodic sentences? As you recall, ending structural units of a sentence (and the entire sentence) with meaningful words is a powerful strategy. Consider this type of sentence structure: "(word position one) (word position two) (word position three) (word position four) (word position five) (word position six) (word position seven) (comma as structural separator) (word position eight) (word position nine) (word position ten) (semicolon as structural separator) (word position eleven) (word position twelve) (word position thirteen) (word position fourteen) (period as structural separator)." The positions of most emphasis, where you should place the meaningful, hard-hitting, essential, emphasis-worthy words, are these: "(word position one) (word position two) (word position three) (word position four) (word position five) (word position six) *(word position seven)* (comma as structural separator) (word position eight) (word position nine) *(word position ten)* (semicolon as structural separator) (word position eleven) (word position twelve) (word position thirteen) *(word position fourteen)* (period as structural separator)."

And JFK follows this rule. For example, look at this segment: "To those new states whom we welcome to the ranks of the *free*, (comma as structural separator) we pledge our word that one form of colonial control shall not have passed away merely to be replaced by a far more iron *tyranny* (period as structural separator)." He places two essential, strategically-selected words, "free" and "tyranny," in the places of most emphasis.

But he takes a step further. Not only does JFK take advantage of the inherent emphasis those positions hold, but he also places words there that contrast with one another: freedom versus tyranny.

And now for metaphor: "those who foolishly sought power by riding the back of the tiger ended up inside." This is figurative language. Are entire nations riding the back of a tiger to seek power? And are those entire nations being eaten by the tiger? As far as I know (and I could be wrong), that's quite impossible (unless you get a very large tiger and a very small nation). But think of the ferocious, powerful, predatory strength of a tiger. That's exactly what patriotic Americans want America to be. Predatory if instigated, but peaceful and noble if not.

KEY INSIGHT:

Many Complex Theories Dressed Up in Complex Terminology Reveal a Single Simple Point.

Our Minds and Memories are Metaphor-Driven. Metaphors Shape Our Worldviews.

PASSAGE #7:

To those peoples in the huts and villages across the globe struggling to break the bonds of mass misery, we pledge our best efforts to help them help themselves, for whatever period is required – not because the Communists may be doing it, not because we seek their votes, but because it is right. If a free society cannot help the many who are poor, it cannot save the few who are rich.

SECRET #68:

Antithetical tricolon, grammatically parallel paradox with symmetrical contrasting words and periodic segments, plus contrasting periodic and mirrored auxiliary words, Virgilian structure-meaning alignment.

He uses templatization: He continues the template established already. This is the third instance. He uses anaphora: "To those..." He uses flowing rhetorical devices: Fragmented alliteration flows into an alliterative couplet ("*b*reak the *b*onds of *m*ass *m*isery"). He uses repetition of words like "globe, right / rights, free, society, etc." He also uses an antithetical tricolon.

What's an antithetical tricolon? Antithesis usually takes the form of "not X, but Y," where X and Y contradict each other. A tricolon is a sentence including a list of three. JFK used both in this sentence: "not because the Communists may be doing it (tricolon part one), not because we seek their votes (tricolon part two), but because it is right (tricolon part three)." It is a tricolon antithetical sentence that takes the form "not X, not Y, but Z." This intensifies the antithesis and contrast while creating rhythm.

Next up, a grammatically parallel paradox with symmetrical contrasting words and periodic segments, plus contrasting periodic and mirrored auxiliary words. In a single sentence, JFK uses grammatical parallelism, repeated grammatical structure, paradox (two things going together that seemingly contradict), contrasting words (opposing words), contrasting symmetries (opposing words in the same positions of sequential sentences), periodic segments (particularly meaningful words placed at the ends of structural units in the sentence), contrasting periodic segments (consecutive periodic segments containing contrasting words), mirrored auxiliary words (identical auxiliary words used to solidify and emphasize the paradox, parallelism, and contrast), mirrored meaningful words supporting the parallelism, meaning and structure alignment, floating opposites, connotative contrasting verbs, the life-force eight desires implicitly invoked, and finally, an "if, then" open loop.

Here's the sentence. "If a free society cannot help the many who are poor, it cannot save the few who are rich."

Grammatical parallelism: "If a free (noun) (adverb) (verb) (article) (noun) (pronoun) (verb) (adjective) (separating comma as line of symmetry) (noun) (adverb) (verb) (article) (noun) (pronoun) (verb) (adjective)." The grammatical parallelism is exact and mirrored across the separating comma after the introductory "if a free..."

He uses paradox: "if we can't help the poor, we can't help the rich." Paradox acts as a reframing technique, specifically frame elevation. This technique reverses the relation between item X and Y presented in the alternate or opposing frame (which is often the assumed default position or intellectual status quo). It zooms out, presenting an old subject from a new perspective, offering an alternative to the status-quo perspective.

He uses antithetical words: "many" and "poor" versus "few" and "rich." And he places them in symmetrical positions: "(noun) one (adverb) two (verb) three (article) four (noun) five (*many*)(pronoun) six (verb) seven (adjective) eight *(poor)*(separating comma as line of symmetry) (noun) one (adverb) two (verb) three (article) four (noun) five *(few)*(pronoun) six (verb) seven (adjective) eight *(rich)*."

The symmetrical positions of the two pairs of contrasting words are also periodic: "If a free society cannot help the many who are poor (position of emphasis at end of segment), it cannot save the few who are rich (position of emphasis at end of sentence)." The contrasting words hold positions of periodic emphasis. Why? To embolden and emphasize the contrast between them; between the few poor and the many rich.

And the auxiliary words mirror to support the grammatical parallelism: "*cannot* help *the* many *who are* poor" and "*cannot* save *the* few *who are* rich." This interweaving of mirrored auxiliary words with opposing, paradoxical, contrasting meaningful words thrills. It builds rhythm and satisfying symmetry, and it emboldens the paradox and contrast.

Now, this next bit might be a little farfetched. So, I refuse to say this is a deliberate choice JFK made. It might be. Meaning and structure alignment comes from Virgilian poetry. The arrangement of the sentence mirrors the meaning and sentiment. The sentiment is that "helping the many poor comes first." And is it a coincidence that helping the many poor literally comes first in the structure of the sentence? Is it a coincidence that the many poor literally come before the few rich? Maybe. Or maybe not.

But the floating or coupled opposites certainly represent deliberate intent. "Poor" and "rich" is the first set of opposites. "Many" and "few" is the second set of opposites. "Many poor" and "few rich" form floating opposites. Two layers of contrasts float in the two sections of the sentence, balancing it out.

Connotative verbs with contrasting connotations tie into this as well. "If a free society cannot *help* the many who are poor, it cannot *save* the few who are rich." Why is verb one "help" and verb two "save?" Because of the associated connotations. "Help" is to give a gentle boost. "Save" is to prevent from total destruction. And it implies that the total destruction of the rich depends on whether or not the free society can gently help the poor. Poor not helped? Rich totally destroyed. This is the subtext of the verbs.

Now this is a rhetorical analysis, not a historical one, but the message of these verbs is particularly pertinent given the historical context. And it implicitly invokes the following italicized human desires (for both the many poor and the few rich): survival, enjoyment of life, life extension; enjoyment of food and beverages; freedom from fear, pain, and danger; comfortable living conditions; to be superior, winning, keeping up with the Joneses; care and protection of loved ones; social approval.

This sentence also acts as a micro-open loop. A micro-open loop opens and closes in the same sentence. In this case, the segment to the left of the comma opens it, and the segment to the right of the comma closes it. In fact, all "if X, then Y" structures inherently act as open loops. They instantly grab audience attention. Why? Because the "if X" demands the "then Y." And when you open the curiosity loop, the "if X," the audience needs to hear the "then Y" to satisfy their curiosity. "What will happen if we can't help the many poor? Tell us!"

One last thing: "...help them help themselves." Enveloped phonetic repetition. It's brilliant. And simple. And baffling. And it sounds incredible. It's rhythmic. It builds cadence. It is incredibly politically savvy, quickly appeasing both liberals and conservatives. It is intellectually challenging. And it just sounds cool.

PASSAGE #8:

To our sister republics south of our border, we offer a special pledge – to convert our good words into good deeds – in a new alliance for progress – to assist free men and free governments in casting off the chains of poverty. But this peaceful revolution of hope cannot become the prey of hostile powers. Let all our neighbors know that we shall join with them to oppose aggression or subversion anywhere in the Americas. And let every other power know that this Hemisphere intends to remain the master of its own house.

SECRET #69:

Template-breaking pattern-interrupts creating structure-meaning alignment, triple repeating attached adjectives, XX1, YY2, ZZ3 constructions, in-text analysis, auxiliary continuity, percussive rhythm versus alliterative flow, letter-level flow, building a thematic pyramid, empowering a narrative with high-stakes language, life-force eight desires, synthesizing tangential, winding, parenthetical sentences, nested to statements.

In this passage, JFK continues the established template. He continues repetition: "our, we, pledge, good, alliance, free, government, hope, peace, revolution, powers, hostile, oppose, neighbors, friends," and motifs of chains and bondage. He continues using fragmented alliteration and symmetrical auxiliary words: "*our sister* republics *south* of *our* border*."

So, what's new? Interestingly enough, JFK slightly breaks from the templatization. This creates emphasis. If you repeat X, the first Y garners emphasis. "X, X, X, X, Y." The first item breaking away from the preceding pattern announces itself.

And the established pattern of this template is "to (group), we pledge (pledge)." But in this section, he makes it "we offer a special pledge." Using "we pledge" to open the pledge paradigm for all the previous groups but "we offer a special pledge" to open this pledge paradigm slightly breaks away from a pattern. Not only is it stated as a special pledge, but its gentle breaking of a preceding pattern actually renders it grammatically and rhetorically special. This acts as a form of meaning and structure alignment. He doesn't just say the pledge is special: he uses a breakaway phrase to emphasize this particular pledge and render it aesthetically special.

JFK also uses repeated attached adjectives, three times. One time is perhaps a coincidence. Three times is clearly intentional. "*Our* sister republics south of *our* border... convert our *good* words into *good* deeds... assist *free* men and *free* governments."

And these were all consecutive: "To our sister republics south of our border, we offer a special pledge – to convert our good words into good deeds – in a new alliance for progress – to assist free men and free governments in casting off the chains of poverty." And not only did he arrange the three pairs of attached adjectives in a rough sequence, but he also chose thematically relevant attached adjectives he also repeated throughout the speech. "Our" represents the theme of American solidarity. "Good" represents the theme of what

America supposedly stands for. "Free" represents the theme of a core American value.

Why did he do this? Because while the consecutive device builds rhythm and flow, sounds eloquent, and produces a pleasing cadence, it also emphasizes thematically important qualities.

Now, I'm going to introduce you to in-text analysis. It might bother you, to be honest, but it's how I analyze these passages. Each individual word in this passage may have up to several sentences of analysis.

"To (continued template repeated from previous passages delayed transition that grabs audience attention and is crisp, clear, and commanding) our (inclusive pronoun that emphasizes a shared bond and engages the audience, the first of a pair of repeated attached adjectives, in a sequence of three pairs of attached adjectives) sister (normal attached adjective inserted to build message-nuance; the first word in a fragmented alliterative couplet) republics south (the second word in the fragmented alliterative couplet with sister) of our (inclusive pronoun the second 'our' in a pair of attached adjectives, completing the first of three pairs of attached adjectives) border, we (inclusive pronoun emphasizing American solidarity and invoking team and tribe psychology) offer (connotative verb carrying a connotation of outreach, generosity, and alliance) a special pledge (repetition of the word pledge, use of the word special to connote that the group is particularly valued, slight breakaway from the established template opening the previous passages in order to indicate 'special' with implicit sentence structure) – to convert our (third repetition of the word 'our' so far; inclusive pronoun) good (the first of a pair of attached adjectives, in the second pair of consecutive attached adjectives) words into good (the second good, completing the second pair of repeated attached adjectives in the set of three pairs) deeds – in a new (repetition of the word new, emphasizing a particular theme and building continuity throughout all passages) alliance (repetition of the word alliance, emphasizing another theme that's repeated throughout the text) for progress (repetition of the word progress, emphasizing another theme in this parenthetical insertion; JFK tied together three sub-themes into one overarching theme by repeating their representative words in close sequence) – to (repeated auxiliary word, which we'll talk about out-of-text as it gets too grainy in-text) assist free (repetition of the word free which is thematically relevant introduction of the first attached adjective in the third and final pair of consecutive pairs of attached adjectives) men and free (the second attached adjective completing the final pair of three consecutive pairs of attached adjectives) governments in casting (storytelling and imagery transmission performed through one of the best mediums, bold and clear action verbs like this previous word) off the chains (bold, evocative, and connotative imagery; figurative and metaphorical language; not phonetically fragmented alliteration because 'c' and 'ch' are phonetically different) of (repeated auxiliary word) poverty (previously repeated and periodic motif of poverty once again repeated and once again periodic). But (delayed transition) this peaceful (repeated word; word representative of a sub-theme) revolution (repeated word, representative of a sub-theme) of hope (repeated word; word representative of a sub-theme the third word in a sequence of three words that are both repeated and representative of sub-themes; completion of a sequence of such words to tie together multiple sub-themes into one unifying theme; the second such sequence in this passage) cannot (repeated auxiliary verb crisp, clear, commanding action verb story progression through verbs, or action words) become the prey (language of danger setting stakes) of (repeated auxiliary words) hostile (repeated word) powers (repeated word periodic sentence). Let (repeated auxiliary word, storytelling and message progression through action verbs, delayed transition opening an anaphora paradigm built on 'let') all (outwardly inclusive: inclusive to the people outside the audience which has already been 'teamed') our (inwardly inclusive: inclusive to the audience, or the 'American team' established through repeated inwardly exclusive pronouns; repeated word) neighbors (repeated word) know (story progression through verbs) that we (inclusive pronoun) shall (repeated auxiliary word; non-pedestrian alternative to the common 'should,' more forceful alternative to 'should,' more elevated alternative than 'should,' more connotative of a goal-setting leader than 'should') join (connotative of team evocative of solidarity) with them to oppose aggression or subversion anywhere in the Americas (too much packed into this whole sentence for a clear in-text analysis, see out of text). And (delayed transition) let (continuation of 'let' anaphora paradigm) every (outwardly inclusive) other power (repeated word) know (repeated action verb) that this (alliterative couplet of auxiliary words) Hemisphere intends to remain the master of its own house."

Perhaps the following visual format is easier to parse.

"To (continued template repeated from previous passages delayed transition that grabs audience attention and is crisp, clear, and commanding) our (inclusive pronoun that emphasizes a shared bond and engages the audience, the first of a pair of repeated attached adjectives, in a sequence of three pairs of attached adjectives) sister (normal attached adjective inserted to build message-nuance; the first word in a fragmented alliterative couplet) republics south (the second word in the fragmented alliterative couplet with sister) of our (inclusive pronoun the second 'our' in a pair of attached adjectives, completing the first of three pairs of attached adjectives) border, we (inclusive pronoun emphasizing American solidarity and invoking team and tribe psychology) offer (connotative verb carrying a connotation of outreach, generosity, and alliance) a special pledge (repetition of the word pledge, use of the word special to connote that the group is particularly valued, slight breakaway from the established template opening the previous passages in order to indicate 'special' with implicit sentence structure) – to convert our (third repetition of the word 'our' so far; inclusive pronoun) good (the first of a pair of attached adjectives, in the second pair of consecutive attached adjectives) words into good (the second good, completing the second pair of repeated attached adjectives in the set of three pairs) deeds – in a new (repetition of the word new, emphasizing a particular theme and building continuity throughout all passages) alliance (repetition of the word alliance, emphasizing another theme that's repeated throughout the text) for progress (repetition of the word progress, emphasizing another theme in this parenthetical insertion; JFK tied together three sub-themes into one overarching theme by repeating their representative words in close sequence) – to (repeated auxiliary word, which we'll talk about out-of-text as it gets too grainy in-text) assist free (repetition of the word free which is thematically relevant introduction of the first attached adjective in the third and final pair of consecutive pairs of attached adjectives) men and free (the second attached adjective completing the final pair of three consecutive pairs of attached adjectives) governments in casting (storytelling and imagery transmission performed through one of the best mediums, bold and clear action verbs like this previous word) off the chains (bold, evocative, and connotative imagery; figurative and metaphorical language; not phonetically fragmented alliteration because 'c' and 'ch' are phonetically different) of (repeated auxiliary word) poverty (previously repeated and periodic motif of poverty once again repeated and once again periodic). But (delayed transition) this peaceful (repeated word; word representative of a sub-theme) revolution (repeated word; word representative of a sub-theme) of hope (repeated word; word representative of a sub-theme the third word in a sequence of three words that are both repeated and representative of sub-themes; completion of a sequence of such words to tie together multiple sub-themes into one unifying theme; the second such sequence in this passage) cannot (repeated auxiliary verb crisp, clear, commanding action verb story progression through verbs, or action words) become the prey (language of danger setting stakes) of (repeated auxiliary words) hostile (repeated word) powers (repeated word periodic sentence). Let (repeated auxiliary word, storytelling and message progression through action verbs, delayed transition opening an anaphora paradigm built on 'let') all (outwardly inclusive: inclusive to the people outside the audience which has already been 'teamed') our (inwardly inclusive: inclusive to the audience, or the 'American team' established through repeated inwardly exclusive pronouns; repeated word) neighbors (repeated word) know (story progression through verbs) that we (inclusive pronoun) shall (repeated auxiliary word; non-pedestrian alternative to the common 'should,' more forceful alternative to 'should,' more elevated alternative than 'should,' more connotative of a goal-setting leader than 'should') join (connotative of team evocative of solidarity) with them to oppose aggression or subversion anywhere in the Americas (too much packed into this whole sentence for a clear in-text analysis, see out of text). And (delayed transition) let (continuation of 'let' anaphora paradigm) every (outwardly inclusive) other power (repeated word) know (repeated action verb) that this (alliterative couplet of auxiliary words) Hemisphere intends to remain the master of its own house."

What's the advantage of in-text analysis? It lets us get incredibly granular, giving every word the close attention it deserves. And it can get even deeper than this previous example.

So, what's the advantage of out-of-text analysis? It lets us see the big picture and identify big patterns that aren't visible if we zoom too far in. Thus, I prefer doing both.

In-text can be hard to read, and overwhelming for people who don't devote their lives to this. Thus, I do in-text in my head as I write the out-of-text analysis out for you. I just wanted to expose you to the in-text strategy for this passage.

From this passage, what techniques belong in an out-of-text analysis? First, repeated auxiliary words. Every time a speaker or writer uses an auxiliary word, they confront a choice between a set of different options; a set of different auxiliary words presenting the same meaning. For a speech like this one, using the same auxiliary words whenever possible works. If there are ten possible purposes you need auxiliary words to fulfill in your speech, you should use one and only one auxiliary word to fulfill each of those ten purposes. Repeating auxiliary words instead of constantly shifting out new ones produces continuity, structure, and clarity. Not repeating auxiliary words confuses the audience, muddies the message, hurts continuity, and makes the speech seem "all over the place."

WHY IMPACTFUL SPEAKERS OPTIMIZE THE SMALL DETAILS

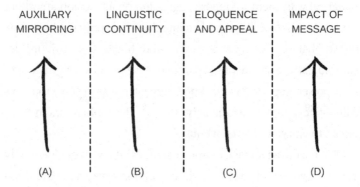

FIGURE 34: As you apply auxiliary mirroring, the perception of linguistic continuity in your speech rises, increasing its eloquence and appeal, which raises its overall persuasive impact on the audience.

KEY INSIGHT:

You Must Pay Attention to the Unimportant Words Only to Guarantee They Don't Take Your Audience's Attention Away from the Important Ones. Make it Easy for Your Audience to Pay Small Mind to Small Matters.

For example, JFK needs auxiliary words to connect an actor (usually "we") to an action: (actor) (auxiliary word) (action). So almost every time this need presents itself, he fulfills it with the same word: "shall." It's predictable. And auxiliary words should almost always be predictable. Remember: Auxiliary words should not distract from the meaningful words, but support them. And constantly using different auxiliary words to fulfill the same purpose distracts. Using "uniformed auxiliaries" creates a sense of efficiency and eloquence, promoting the impression that the speech is tight and focused on what really matters, containing no unnecessary word.

Now, we turn to another element that in-text analysis is no good for: Percussive rhythm versus alliterative flow.

An example of percussive rhythm is this: "...to convert our good words into good deeds..."

A few core elements create percussive rhythm.

Consonance: the recurrence of similar sounds, especially consonants, in close proximity.

Assonance: a resemblance in the sounds of words and syllables either between their vowels or between their consonants. (This is the "official" definition: I use consonance for consonants and assonance for vowels – simple as that).Consonating consonants enveloping assonating vowels.

Starting and ending words with the punchy consonants

Starting the next word with the last letter in the previous word.

Ending a word with the first letter in the word before it.

Consonance particularly of punchy, percussive consonants.

Short, snappy words.

Symmetrical noun forms.

Repetition.

Syllabic symmetry.

Let me prove it mathematically if you're skeptical.

Consonance of a set of punchy, percussive consonants. Here's the consonant map of that segment: "TTGDDTGDDD." 7 out of 8, or 87.5% of the words in the sentence, had a punchy consonant dominating the phonetics of the word.

Assonance: 7 out of 8, or 87.5% of the words in that segment had an "oo" or "o" sound.

Consonating consonants enveloping assonating vowels; of the "TGD" consonants that dominate the segment enveloping the "oo" or "o" vowel sounds that assonate. "*To convert our good words into good* deeds." TooToGooDoDToGooD. This pattern of assonating "oo" sounds between consonating "TGD" consonants appears in 6 out of 8, or 75% of the words in this sentence. And one of the two times this pattern of consonating consonants enveloping assonating vowels breaks is to satisfy another one of the percussive rhythm requirements.

Starting or ending words with the punchy consonants: 7 out of 8, or 87.5% of the words in this phrase start or end with the "TGD" consonants. 4 out of 8, or 50% start and end with them (ignoring the pluralic "s" added on to them).

Starting the next word with the last letter in the previous word: "goo*d d*eeds."

Ending a word with the first letter in the word before it: "*t*o conver*t.*"

Consonance particularly of punchy, percussive consonants: we briefly talked about this, but "TGD" are all punchy and percussive. How do you know? Try saying them. You'll notice a mini "explosion" in your throat. The letters P, C, and K are similar. Compare this explosive feeling with the feeling of saying non-percussive consonants, like "M," or "N."

Short, snappy words: 6 out of 8, or 75% of the words in this sentence are one syllable long. The average length of the words in this sentence is 4.25. The 2 words that aren't one syllable are only two syllables.

Symmetrical noun forms: "words ... deeds."

Repetition: "good ... good."

Syllabic symmetry: "good (one syllable) words (one syllable) into (two syllables) good (one syllable) deeds (one syllable)." 1 1 2 1 1, with the two-syllable word as the line of symmetry. This sentence is also symmetrical in some other ways: "good (one syllable, four letters) words (one syllable, five letters) into (two syllables, four letters) good (one syllable, four letters) deeds (one syllable, five letters)."

Syllabic symmetry: 1 1 2 1 1

Word-length symmetry: *4 5 4 4 5*, with the dividing two-syllable word bifurcating the sentence into two "4 5" length segments.

Now, why use percussive rhythm at all?

It is captivating.

It is memorable.

It is attention-grabbing.

It is direct.

It is clear.

It is forceful.

It is distinct.

But this is all about percussive rhythm versus alliterative flow, not just percussive rhythm as it stands alone.

Note that some elements of percussive rhythm also create alliterative flow. The key distinction is this: which set of elements dominates the sentence?

So, let's talk about this line: "With them to oppose aggression or subversion anywhere in the..."

"With them" creates th-th flow.

"Them to" creates an alliterative couplet.

"To oppose" creates o-o flow and o-oppo assonance.

"Oppose aggression" creates e-a flow, vowel to vowel.

"Aggression subversion" creates a fragmented reverse alliterative couplet: sion-sion.

"Oppose aggression or" creates a fragmented alliterative couplet.

"Oppose... or oppose aggression or subversion" creates a fragmented alliterative couplet nested in a fragmented reverse alliterative couplet. These two couplets fragment each other.

"Anywhere in" creates e-i flow, vowel to vowel.

And consider the absence of the most important percussive element: explosive, percussive consonants.

In the percussive "hard-rhythm" sentence, 11 out of 34 letters are hard, percussive consonants. That's roughly 32.4%.

In the alliterative "soft-flow" sentence, 9 out of 51 letters are hard, percussive consonants. That's 17.6% of the letters. But the "th" sound (with them) is softer and less percussive than the "t" sound, so that becomes 7 out of 51 letters, or 13.7%. And the percussive consonants in "oppose aggression" are coupled up, like so: PP, GG. Phonetically, PP and GG sound the same as P and G. So that becomes 5 out of 51 letters that are truly *phonetically* percussive consonants, or under 10%.

The sentence with percussive rhythm has well over three times as many hard, percussive consonants as the sentence with soft, alliterative flow.

Hopefully after all this numeric evidence, you see the intent and deliberation behind high-stakes speech-writing.

Vowels and alliterative devices dominate sentences with alliterative flow, which contain fewer percussive consonants.

The word "anywhere" seems to just flow. Why? Because it contains no percussive consonants whatsoever. The word does not deliver a series of forceful, hard-hitting, explosive punches. It is one drawn out note.

JFK deliberately uses both percussive rhythm and alliterative flow. And that's perfect. Using percussive rhythm constantly is too percussive. Using alliterative flow constantly is too soft and flowy.

So, what does JFK do? He uses both, and bounces back and forth between them. He relaxes us with soft-flow, and then gives us a jarring shock with hard-rhythm. That's mastery.

Further, JFK ties themes together in this passage. He presents individual themes, and then attaches them together to form overarching, unifying themes. Such unification occurs three times in this passage.

Previously in his speech, he presented a set of themes by repeating certain words: "new, alliance, progress, free, peace, revolution, hope." Thematic words of this stripe tend to be broad, aspirational, vague, abstract conceptual ideas or principles. Words like "White House" are not thematic words. Concrete words like "White House," which refers to a specific and distinct building, tend to act as symbolic words, symbolizing the aforementioned thematic words. What does "new" symbolize? Hard to say. What does "freedom" symbolize? Hard to say. What does "hope" symbolize? Hard to say. They are not principally symbolic: they are what symbols point to, not symbols in and of themselves. What does "White House?" symbolize? Renewal, freedom, and hope.

Look how he ties separate sub-themes into unifying themes in this passage: "*new alliance* for *progress*... *free* men and *free government*... *peaceful revolution* of *hope*."

We talked about anaphora and templatization before. We see some more in this passage: anaphora of "let" and templatization of "let (group) know (insert message to group phrased as knowledge)."

JFK does something captivating in this passage. He speaks in the language of fear, loss, and danger. Phrases like chains of poverty, prey of hostile powers, and aggression or subversion trigger these emotions.

Why is this so powerful? Because JFK (like any good speaker) is building a narrative. And a narrative only works if the audience is the hero in the narrative and there are high stakes. If there's nothing at stake, if there's no threat or danger to them, if there's nothing to overcome, nobody cares. And with these phrases, JFK sets clear and important stakes. These also connect to some of the life-force eight desires: survival, enjoyment of life, life extension; enjoyment of food and beverages; freedom from fear, pain, and danger; comfortable living conditions; to be superior, winning, keeping up with the Joneses; care and protection of loved ones; social approval.

THE KEY TO MASSIVE PERSUASIVE FORCE: HUMAN DESIRE

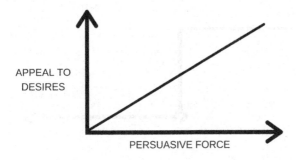

FIGURE 35: As you tie your message to the desires of your audience members (of which the life force eight are a small but powerful sampling), the persuasive force of your message rises significantly.

Now, JFK uses parenthetical, tangential, and winding sentences. He deviates from a straight line that takes you directly from A to B, but he also completes synthesis from A to B and achieves cogency of speech. He uses complex sentence structure, with twists and folds, sub-enumerations, sub-points and parentheticals, but he still wraps up his initial thought and maintains clarity. Parentheticals and tangents tend to demolish most speakers, particularly in extemporaneous or impromptu speech. Avoid them. But note this as an example of a speaker successful pulling them off.

HOW TANGENTS BLUR, WEAKEN, AND DILUTE A MESSAGE

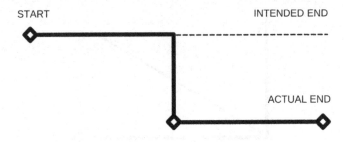

FIGURE 36: Tangents occur when you take a detour from the intended path of a sentence and arrive at a different, unplanned, non-essential end.

HOW PARANTHETICALS DIMINISH THE CORE MESSAGE

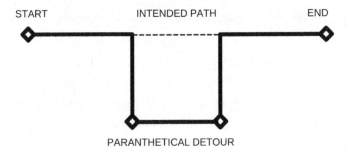

FIGURE 37: Parentheticals occur when you inject non-essential information in the path of a sentence, taking a longer path to the same end.

A VISUALIZATION OF LONG, WINDING SENTENCES

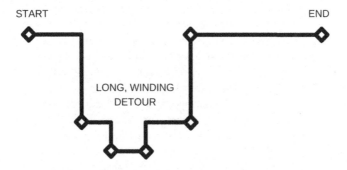

FIGURE 38: Long, winding sentences often use frequent tangents and parentheticals, sometimes chaining them together and producing a tangent off of a tangent, or a parenthetical in a parenthetical, etc.

THE DANGER OF TANGENTS AND PARANTHETICALS

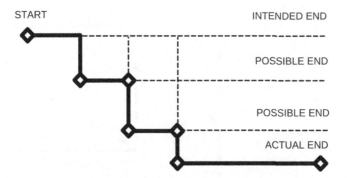

FIGURE 39: Not managing tangents and parentheticals can ruin your message. Here, the speaker takes three tangents, arriving far removed from the intended purpose of the sentence. It is the difference between "Denmark is not a good economic model for the United States because it is an internally homogenous economy" and "Denmark is

not a good economic model for the United States because – by the way, it has its own set of problems (tangent one) – all countries have advantages and disadvantages (tangent two) – the United States spends lots of money in NATO to protect Denmark unnecessarily (tangent three) and this sort of explains the situation at hand." Each tangent provided an opportunity to loop back into the initial sentence (the vertical dotted lines) or to continue on to a potential end that would have been closer to the initial intended end (the horizontal dotted lines). For example, returning to the initial sentence after the first tangent would have sounded like this: "Denmark is not a good economic model for the United States because – by the way, it has its own set of problems (tangent one) – and is not a good model because it is an internally homogenous economy." Reaching a conclusion closer to the intended end (following the first of the two horizontal lines labeled "possible end") would have sounded like this: "Denmark is not a good economic model for the United States because – by the way, it has its own set of problems like massive taxation, which we want to avoid here."

THE BIGGER THE DETOUR, THE WORSE THE MESSAGE

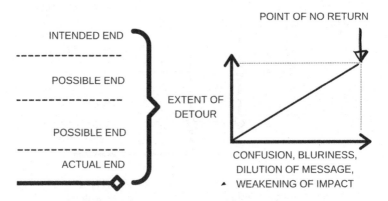

FIGURE 40: As the distance between the intended end and the actual end rises, the confusion, blurriness, dilution of the message, and weakening of impact rise. Eventually, the speaker hits a "point of no return" where one of a set of

possibilities occurs: they stop talking, they stop talking and apologize (I've seen it happen multiple times), they recollect themselves after a pause and continue to the next sentence, someone interrupts the and takes charge of the conversation, etc.

HOW TO ACHIEVE CLARITY, FOCUS, AND COGENCY

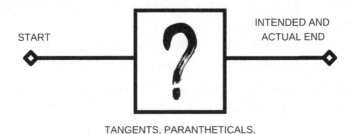

FIGURE 41: A sentence achieves synthesis when its intended end is its actual end, no matter what goes on in between the beginning and the end. Achieving synthesis produces a focused, tight, clear, logical message.

JFK also uses "nested to statements." This creates a powerful rhythm, moving the speech forward and creating narrative momentum. "To our sister republics south of our border, we offer a special pledge – to convert our good words into good deeds – in a new alliance for progress – to assist free men and free governments in casting off the chains of poverty."

PASSAGE #9:

To that world assembly of sovereign states, the United Nations, our last best hope in an age where the instruments of war have far outpaced the instruments of peace, we renew our pledge of support

– to prevent it from becoming merely a forum for invective – to strengthen its shield of the new and the weak – and to enlarge the area in which its writ may run.

SECRET #70:

Consecutive attached adjective (double attached adjectives) with multiple symmetries, the two-prong attached adjective algorithm.

He continues the "to (group) we pledge (pledge)" template, but he also modifies it slightly. He continues to repeat certain words: "world, states, our, hope, age, war, peace, pledge, support, strengthen, new" etc. He continues using nested "to" statements to build rhythm and speak efficiently. He continues to use intertwined fragmented alliterative couplets: "*i*n *w*hich *i*ts *w*rit." This phrase also packs together assonance and consonance, plus many other phonetic strategies. Just listen to how satisfying the phrase sounds. He continues fragmented alliterative couplets: "strengthen its shield." He continues micro-parallelism: "the new and the weak." He continues inclusive pronouns. He continues contrasts: "the instruments of war have far outpaced the instruments of peace." This is also micro-parallelism in the form (noun) of (noun): "instruments of war... instruments of peace," and he couples it with strict word-level parallelism, repeating the word "instruments." He continues periodic sentences. He continues elevated, connotative, and evocative language.

In this section, he truly just continues what he's been doing.

An interesting turn of phrase is "last best." These consecutive attached adjectives achieve symmetry in many ways: they produce reverse alliteration (they rhyme), they contain four letters, they include one syllable, they possess similar forms ("consonant, vowel, s, t") and they both quickly deliver new pieces of information about the subject to which they are attached. Further, they exemplify a play on a strategy you already know: the attached adjective algorithm. Perform it, but add two adjectives before the modified noun. This allows you additional opportunity for creating aesthetic appeal: the adjectives can mesh with each other and the noun they modify.

PASSAGE #10:

Finally, to those nations who would make themselves our adversary, we offer not a pledge but a request: that both sides begin anew the quest for peace, before the dark powers of destruction unleashed by science engulf all humanity in planned or accidental self-destruction.

SECRET #71:

Climactic language, "different than the rest" emphasis, "best for last" emphasis, elevated grammar and simple words, the peak-end rule.

The past five or so passages clearly exemplify the strategy of separation of concerns. It produces a clear and compelling structure. It builds rhythm. It establishes a familiar template: "to (group) we pledge (pledge)" and embeds new information in a familiar template.

Each group JFK wants to make a pledge to gets a clear and direct introduction. And he just moves through them in sequence. He separates them into their own distinct segments of speech; into their separate units of meaning.

He also combines the "best for last" and "different from the rest" structure approaches. These strategies resemble periodic sentences. In speech (and probably many other domains), what comes last and what breaks away from a preceding pattern receives emphasis. "Finally (best for last), to those nations who would make themselves our adversary, we offer not a pledge but a request (different than the rest)…"

"DIFFERENT THAN THE REST" CONTEXTUAL EMPHASIS

FIGURE 42: The different item stands out.

"BEST FOR LAST" CONTEXTUAL EMPHASIS

FIGURE 43: The last item stands out.

HOW TO COMBINE TWO MODES OF CONTEXTUAL EMPHASIS

FIGURE 44: JFK combined the two modes of contextual emphasis by placing the item he wanted to emphasize last and clothing it differently than the items around it.

He left this group for last, emphasizing it and raising its perceived importance. He also broke away from a familiar pattern, which does the same. And no wonder: This particular part of his message to this particular group is particularly important.

Speaking of periodic sentences and segments, this section is full of them. He places the following words in periodic positions: "adversary, request, peace, self-destruction."

And he also uses contrasting periodicals (again). "Peace" versus "destruction."

Despite using elevated grammar, JFK manages to communicate with relatively simple words. Most of the words he uses are short, snappy, and contain a small number of syllables. Despite that, they are still elevated, evocative, and connotative. It's a delicate balance. And JFK accomplishes it extremely well.

But here's the key point to note in this passage: JFK's speech contains two climaxes. It's unusual. In fact, it's not even really recommended. But he does it and does it well.

This passage produces the first climax. Best for last structural prioritization, breakaway structural prioritization, and extremely climactic language create the climactic mood.

What defines climactic language? While we possess multiple forms of climactic language, this particular form carries the following distinct characteristics.

Stakes: The language sets high stakes.

Danger: The language portrays danger.

Emotional arousal: The language raises emotional arousal.

Urgency: The language implies or explicitly presents a time limit.

Goal: The language establishes a goal.

Enemy: The language presents an enemy or threat.

Spread: The language achieves relevance to a wide group.

Action: The language creates verb-driven momentum.

Paths: The language expresses one bad and one good option.

Real-world purpose: The language serves a real-world purpose.

"...that both sides begin anew the quest for peace (real-world purpose of making an actual request to a foreign power plus the first of two paths), before (urgency plus an implied time limit) the dark powers of destruction (enemy) unleashed (action verb) by science engulf all humanity (wide-relevance) in planned or accidental self-destruction (stakes plus danger plus high-arousal emotion)."

This all has to do with the peak-end rule. People remember the "peak" of an experience (the most intense point) and the "end" of an experience more than anything else. And using these ten components of negative climactic language, JFK placed his peak right here, exactly where he wanted it.

HOW THE PEAK-END RULE GOVERNS MEMORY

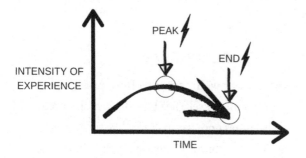

FIGURE 45: People by and large remember a past experience according to their feelings during the moment of peak intensity across the duration of the experience as well as their feelings during the end.

KEY INSIGHT:

"They Forget What You Said, Never How You Made Them Feel," Goes the Common Quote.

Yes... Specifically How You Made Them Feel at the Moment of Peak Intensity and At the End.

PASSAGE #11:

We dare not tempt them with weakness. For only when our arms are sufficient beyond doubt can we be certain beyond doubt that they will never be employed.

SECRET #72:

Percussive rhythm, t-t flow, inherent t-t flow, anastrophe.

The paradox announces itself. See how distinct and predictable his speaking style becomes once we analyze it like this?

Paradox, antithesis, contrast, delayed transitions, inclusive pronouns, alliterative couplets, percussive rhythm, grammatical parallelism, etc. All of this represents part of a set of characteristics that defines JFK's rhetorical approach (and don't forget, when I say "JFK," I mean "JFK and his team of speech writers.)"

We see it now, and we've seen it before too. And we will absolutely see it more. The paradox produces a particularly powerful effect because of the repetitive key phrase "beyond doubt." And the phonetics of this segment produce a similarly powerful rhetorical impact: "...not tempt them with weakness." Why? Two principal reasons account for the rhetorical force: percussive rhythm and t-t flow ("no*t t*empt" and "temp*t t*hem," as well as the t-t- flow inherent in the word "*t*emp*t*.")

But since we've done sentences like this before, I challenge you to find the other phonetic and rhetorical components contributing to that segment's power.

Now, let's talk about anastrophe. "Anastro-what?" you ask. Here it is: "We *dare not* tempt them with weakness." It's transposition of normal word order. It usually involves omitting some auxiliary words (which is good). The proper, "normal" word choice is this: "We do not dare to tempt them with weakness." But the anastrophe of "dare not" flows better, sounds better, and exudes more eloquence. "Do not dare to" versus "dare not."

PASSAGE #12:

But neither can two great and powerful groups of nations take comfort from our present course – both sides overburdened by the cost of modern weapons, both rightly alarmed by the steady spread of the deadly atom, yet both racing to alter that uncertain balance of terror that stays the hand of mankind's final war.

SECRET #73:

Sentence-level anaphora, rhetorical continuity.

Delayed transition to start: "but."

Fragmented alliterative couplet: "great and powerful groups."

Tricolon: "– both sides (...) both rightly (...) yet both."

Periodic segments and ending: "course, weapons, atom, war."

Inclusive pronouns: "our."

Alliterative couplet: "steady spread," plus assonance of "ea" and consonance of "d."

Metaphor: "stays the hand of mankind's final war."

Repeated auxiliary words: "yet both racing to alter *that* uncertain balance of terror *that* stays..."

Tricolon enumeratio: "two great and powerful nations – both (enumeration of qualities), both (enumeration of qualities), yet both (enumeration of qualities)."

Sentence-level anaphora: "both (...) both (...) both (...)"

Attached adjectives: "modern weapons, rightly alarmed, steady spread, deadly atom, uncertain balance, final war."

Evocative, connotative, and elevated language.

Templatization: "both (insert quality)."

PASSAGE #13:

So let us begin anew – remembering on both sides that civility is not a sign of weakness, and sincerity is always subject to proof. Let us never negotiate out of fear. But let us never fear to negotiate.

SECRET #74:

Long-form consonance, layered paradox, antithesis, and chiasmus, subtext.

Repetition of "let us begin anew" from a previous passage.

Parenthetical insertions.

Repetition of "both sides."

Repetition of "weakness."

Anaphora of "let us."

Long-form consonance: "is not a sign of weakness, and sincerity is always subject to proof."

Paradox, antithesis, and chiasmus: "Let us never negotiate out of fear. But let us never fear to negotiate."

The repetition is intentional, to accomplish a purpose. All of this is intentional and purposeful. "Both sides." Why does he repeat that phrase so often? Think about the message it implies: "Listen, it's not just you who is threatening to destroy the world and all of humanity. It's me too. Let's both sit down and figure this out. We both have a part to play. Let's work together."

PASSAGE #14:

Let both sides explore what problems unite us instead of belaboring those problems which divide us.

SECRET #75:

The rhetorical stack.

Paradox.

Anaphora.

Antithesis.

Contrast.

Repetition.

Outwardly inclusive pronouns.

Delayed transitions.

Grammatical parallelism.

This is a common mold for JFK. It is the most distinctive, memorable quality of his speech. And it motivates mention of the rhetorical stack. Do you need to master each and every secret in this book? Or in all of my books? No. You need to develop a rhetorical stack: master ten or so strategies. But I mean really master them. Master them to the point of complete impromptu fluency. Select strategies that come easily to you and strategies that complement each other.

WHY THE RHETORICAL STACK IS THE KEY TO MASTERY

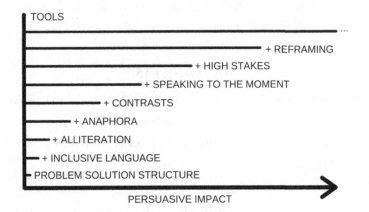

FIGURE 46: Stacking rhetorical tools, particularly rhetorical tool that complement each other, produces non-linear increases in your persuasive impact.

Let's zoom out for a moment. JFK is eloquent. And eloquence is good. But eloquence is not random or abstract; instead, eloquence is the result of clear, concrete, deliberate techniques. You can analyze JFK's speech to find those techniques. You can use them to be eloquent, which is good.

Most people think you either have or don't have eloquence. They think certain speakers captivate and engage and speak with eloquence because they just do. They think you either possess eloquence or do not; that eloquence is a random skill.

They are so wrong (as I've proven to you). Just look at this sentence: "Let both sides explore what problems unite us instead of belaboring those problems which divide us." It is eloquent. It has been quoted countless times. People remember it to this day.

You can decode what makes it eloquent, quotable, and memorable. You can break down the sentence into a simple mold. You can then fill that mold with your words. And guess what? As long as you adhere to the restrictions of the original mold, you can be eloquent, quoted, and remembered too.

It gets better: When you compile a list of these molds and master them, speaking with eloquence on command comes easily to you.

PASSAGE #15:

Let both sides, for the first time, formulate serious and precise proposals for the inspection and control of arms – and bring the absolute power to destroy other nations under the absolute control of all nations.

SECRET #76:

In-text-markup analysis.

I introduced you to in-text analysis. I introduced you to out-of-text analysis. Now let me show you in-text-markup analysis.

In-text markup analysis is a form of in-text analysis that doesn't get as granular, serving two functions. First, it identifies larger components of rhetoric. Second, it marks up text using bold, italics, highlighting, letter-case, and underlining to illustrate those larger components of rhetoric.

"Let both sides (anaphora, strategic repetition, delayed transition, and templatization), for the first time, formulate SeriouS and preciSe propoSalS for the inSpection and control of armS (fragmented alliteration, consonance, and nested alliterative couplets) – and bring the absolute power to destroy other nations under the absolute control of all nations."

Enveloped phonetic repetition strikes again. We've seen this with "help them help themselves," and we'll see it again later: the repetition of the entirety of a word within a closely subsequent word. "*For* the first time, *for*mulate..." It is one of the most advanced, expert strategies for creating attention-grabbing rhythm.

PASSAGE #16:

Let both sides seek to invoke the wonders of science instead of its terrors. Together let us explore the stars, conquer the deserts, eradicate disease, tap the ocean depths, and encourage the arts and commerce.

SECRET #77:

In-text-markup as a window to letter-level flow.

Let both sides (anaphora, strategic repetition, delayed transition, and templatization) seek to invoke the wonderS of Science inStead of itS terrorS. Together (outwardly inclusive politically savvy language) let us (anaphora) explore the stars (enumeratio of invoking the wonders of science in the grammatically parallel form of verb the noun), conquer the deserts, eradicate disease (slight breakaway from the pattern), tap the ocean depths, and encourage the arts and commerce.

PASSAGE #17:

Let both sides unite to heed in all corners of the earth the command of Isaiah – to "undo the heavy burdens... and to let the oppressed go free."

SECRET #78:

Nuance and supportive information buttressing a main message, borrowed biblical eloquence, religious motifs and religious imagery, biblical quotes supporting the message, biblical quotes providing rhetorical symmetry with the passage itself.

JFK seems to add words that don't contribute to his main message but that add nuance and supportive information.

His main message is as follows: "Let both sides heed the command of Isaiah – to 'undo the heavy burdens... and to let the oppressed go free.'"

His main message plus the added nuance and supportive information is as follows: "Let both sides unite to heed in all corners of the earth the command of Isaiah – to 'undo the heavy burdens... and to let the oppressed go free.'"

See how those segments don't necessarily make or break the main message, but instead support it and add eloquent nuance? See how those segments do not just support it and add eloquent nuance, but intensify it?

JFK uses biblical references and religious imagery in this segment. This resonated with his audience. JFK selected a quote from a bible verse which repeated some of the same words he's been repeating.

This is not a coincidence. If you only gain one lesson from this analysis, let it be this: Where you once saw coincidence in legendary communication, there is only deliberate intent and intentional strategy woven by the expert hands of an artisan speech writer.

"Undo the heavy burdens... and to let the oppressed go free."

PASSAGE #18:

And if a beachhead of cooperation may push back the jungle of suspicion, let both sides join in creating a new endeavor, not a new balance of power, but a new world of law, where the strong are just and the weak secure and the peace preserved.

SECRET #79:

Metaphorception with grammatically parallel metaphors that contrast and create an if-then open loop, one-third implied and two-thirds explicit parallel form, sounding phonetically "inside out."

JFK uses metaphorception in this passage. It's quite unbelievable. He says the following: "And if (insert metaphor one) may push back (insert metaphor two)" in which metaphor one plus metaphor two, taken together, form a larger metaphor – metaphor three. Let me repeat: Metaphor one plus metaphor two form a larger metaphor three. He builds a metaphor out of metaphors.

Metaphor one: beachhead of cooperation.

Metaphor two: jungle of suspicion.

Metaphor three: beachhead pushing back a jungle. A direct metaphor to the United States establishing beachheads in the pacific theatre of war during World War Two; beachheads established to push back the Japanese-held jungle.

ADVANCED, SUBCONSIOUSLY COMPELLING METAPHORS

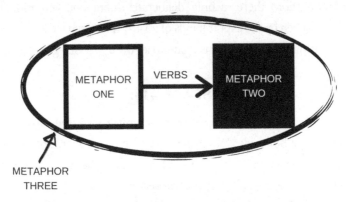

FIGURE 47: JFK delivered a metaphor that acted on another metaphor, which taken as a whole produced a third metaphor. This exemplifies the artistry of eloquence.

See how the two metaphors are not only consecutive, but form a bigger metaphor? See how they make sense at multiple levels of interpretation and analysis and deliver a subconscious, subtextual, subtle message?

Further, the figurative language between metaphors one and two create parallelism in the form (noun) of (noun). A beachhead of cooperation. A jungle of suspicion. They also contrast: "beachhead" versus "jungle," and "cooperation" versus "suspicion." It's a double contrast. Additionally: the metaphors nest within an open loop; an "if X, then Y" open loop envelops them.

In this passage, we see a tricolon continuing anaphora with grammatical parallelism, repetition, periodic segments, and antithesis: "Let both sides (anaphora, strategic repetition, delayed transition, and templatization) join in creating a new endeavor (periodic position, plus tricolon item one), not a new balance of power (periodic position, plus tricolon item two, plus opening of antithesis; 'not X'), but a new world of law (periodic position, plus tricolon item three, plus closing of antithesis; 'but Y')."

We also see parallel structure and strict parallelism (or strict micro-repetition) between two of the three tricolons (the two that are antithetical) in the form new (noun) of (noun): "new balance of power... new world of law."

And this is even more repetition of the word "new," which JFK already repeats abundantly throughout. All of this, taken together, is also enumeratio of the phrase "new endeavor."

"...join in creating a new endeavor, not a new balance of power (enumerated quality one), but a new world of law (enumerated quality two), where the strong are just and the weak secure and the peace preserved (enumerated quality three)."

And this final segment presents its own rhetorical genius: "...where the strong are just and the weak secure and the peace preserved."

"Peace preserved" is an alliterative couplet. It is also polysyndeton, the use of unnecessary conjunctions. "Where the strong are just and the weak secure and the peace preserved." And it is also a psuedo-tricolon in one-third implied and two-third explicit parallel form: "...where the strong are just (item one) and the weak secure (item two) and the peace preserved (item three)."

One-third implied and two-third explicit parallel form?

"Strong are just..." (noun) are (adjective).

"Weak (are) secure..." (noun) (implied "are") (adjective).

"Peace (is) preserved..." (noun) (implied "is") (adjective).

And these implied auxiliary words nest within a sentence that uses polysyndeton, or the statement of implied conjunctions.

So, what's the situation? It's an interesting one. The words usually implied (like "and") are stated. The words usually stated (like "is," and "are,") are implied. That's why this sentence sort of sounds "inside out." Which is a good thing. Why? Because it changes up a pattern. And this holds audience attention.

KEY INSIGHT:

We Are Wired to Notice the New and Forget the Unchanging,

New Means Opportunity or Threat; Potential Gain or Loss.

Unchanging Often Means "No New Gain or Loss Here!"

PASSAGE #19:

All this will not be finished in the first 100 days. Nor will it be finished in the first 1,000 days, nor in the life of this Administration, nor even perhaps in our lifetime on this planet. But let us begin.

SECRET #80:

Rhetorical climax, auxesis.

In-text markup: "All this will not be finished in the first 100 days. Nor will it be finished in the first 1,000 days, nor in the life of this

Administration, nor even perhaps in our lifetime on this planet. But let us begin."

This passage creates a rhetorical climax: arranging words, phrases, or clauses in order of increasing importance or intensity. The term auxesis refers to producing rhetorical climax with sentence clauses.

The previous rhetorical climax of this speech was major and definitive. A series of major structural segments arranged in order of increasing importance created it. Entire passages built the crescendo. On the contrary, this passage represents micro-climax, self-contained within a passage. Segments of a sentence or short sentences create it, not entire passages.

PASSAGE #20:

In your hands, my fellow citizens, more than in mine, will rest the final success or failure of our course. Since this country was founded, each generation of Americans has been summoned to give testimony to its national loyalty. The graves of young Americans who answered the call to service surround the globe.

SECRET #81:

Avoiding counterproductive connotations producing negative subtexts.

Changing one tiny word in this entire passage would have instantly made JFK seem weak and disconnected.

And in this case, it was much easier to get it wrong than to get it right. Check out this word: "In your hands, my fellow citizens, *more* than in mine, will rest the final success or failure of our course."

Saying "not, rather, instead of in," or any similar phrase would have presented a disdainful message to hear from any leader, let alone the leader of the free world. He would be saying "you're responsible for this, not me." Instead, he wisely avoided this huge mistake and said "more than," which means this: "you're primarily responsible for this, but I am right there with you."

PASSAGE #21:

Now the trumpet summons us again – not as a call to bear arms, though arms we need; not as a call to battle, though embattled we are – but a call to bear the burden of a long twilight struggle, year in and year out, 'rejoicing in hope, patient in tribulation' – a struggle against the common enemies of man: tyranny, poverty, disease, and war itself.

KEY INSIGHT:

An Inestimably Significant Amount of Meaning is Buried Below the Surface of Language.

It Is Hidden Away in Subtext, Nuance, and Implication. It Speaks Softly, But It Speaks.

Make Sure It's on Your Side.

SECRET #82:

The VAKOG senses.

What does this passage teach us? It teaches us how to use the VAKOG senses by presenting language stimulating to the following senses...

Visual.

Auditory.

Kinesthetic.

Olfactory.

Gustatory.

In these speeches, the speaker typically goes straight for the visual sense. JFK is no different. Throughout this speech, he consistently uses visually stimulating language. But in this section, he applies the second most compelling kind of sense-driven language: auditory language. He presents the mission as the call of a trumpet, compelling people to the challenge.

Let's cover the rest with in-text-markup analysis.

"Now (delayed transition) the trumpet summons us (alliteration of T, reverse alliteration of T, consonance of M and assonance of U) again – not (antithesis) as a call to bear arms, though arms we need; not as a call to battle, though embattled we are (parallelism) – but (completing antithesis) a call to bear the burden of a long twilight (elevated, visually stimulating, emotionally evocative language) struggle, year in and year out, 'rejoicing in hope, patient in (repetition of verb in) tribulation (parallelism: verb in noun, twice)' – a struggle (repetition of struggle) against the common enemies of man (consonance of M): tyranny, poverty, disease, and war itself."

PASSAGE #22:

Can we forge against these enemies a grand and global alliance, North and South, East and West, that can assure a more fruitful life for all mankind? Will you join in that historic effort?

SECRET #83:

Interrogative cascade, enveloped repetition.

Ending with consecutive rhetorical questions like this, beckoning the audience towards the cause, produces an interrogative cascade.

"North and South, East and West," is both an enumeration and a superabundance (rhetorical addition and expansion).

"Grand and global..." is not just a fragmented alliterative couplet. It's literal repetition of a word. Can you find it? "Grand and global..."

This is why that phrase has such a captivating cadence. "Gr*and* *and* global..." the repeated word gives it a rhythm that is unlike any other strategy we've discussed, and that is unparalleled in its aesthetic appeal. And this is not an accident. Remember "help them help them?" And in the previous passage, "not as a call to *battle*, though em*battle*d?"

PASSAGE #23:

In the long history of the world, only a few generations have been granted the role of defending freedom in its hour of maximum danger. I do not shrink from this responsibility – I welcome it. I do not believe that any of us would exchange places with any other people or any other generation. The energy, the faith, the devotion which we bring to this endeavor will light our country and all who serve it – and the glow from that fire can truly light the world.

SECRET #84:

Opening tricolons.

"In the long history of the world, only a few generations have been granted the role of defending freedom in its hour of maximum danger (lots of assonance, flowing in and out of itself, and enveloping itself). I do not shrink from this responsibility – I welcome it (I assonance). I do not (anaphora) believe that any of us would exchange places with any other people or any other generation (micro-parallelism). The energy, the faith, the devotion (tricolon and asyndeton, missing the and in the final piece of the triad) which we bring to this endeavor will light (il – li) our country and all (fragmented L reverse alliteration) who serve it – and the glow from that fire can truly light (ly – li) the world (massive amount of visually stimulating language and image-based metaphor)."

Tricolons rarely start sentences; they typically end them. Normally, a tricolon occurs like this: "we will win with our energy, our faith, and our devotion," with the sentence ending on the tricolon. But JFK started the sentence with the tricolon, providing a varied turn of phrase.

PASSAGE #24:

And so, my fellow Americans: ask not what your country can do for you – ask what you can do for your country.

SECRET #85:

Double delayed transitions, high word economy.

He started with a double delayed transition: "and so..." Delayed transitions essentially pack a lot of meaning into one word. "And" encapsulates the meaning of the transition "in addition to that..." while "so" encapsulates the meaning of the transition "and therefore..." This provides a rapid, punchy pivot to the new passage.

He followed the delayed transition with an expletive; a short interjection typically (but not always) used to tie the language back to the speaker and the audience: "... my fellow Americans ..."

The remainder of the passage (which is really just a sentence) draws its strength from chiasmus. To review, the complex definition of chiasmus, according to Google Dictionary, is this: "a rhetorical or literary figure in which words, grammatical constructions, or concepts are repeated in reverse order, in the same or a modified form; e.g. 'Poetry is the record of the best and happiest moments of the happiest and best minds.'" And it is chiasmus nested in an antithesis (or perhaps vice-versa). The antithesis? "Ask not X; ask (in the place of a 'but') Y." See how the most famous line in the entire speech, a line remembered by all who heard it, is simply just a bunch of these rhetorical strategies combined with compelling meaning?

KEY INSIGHT:

Great Speech is More Than Just Great Rhetoric. It is Great Rhetoric Plus Great Meaning.

And of the Two, Great Meaning Carries More Greatness. Rhetoric Serves Meaning, Not the Reverse.

PASSAGE #25:

"My fellow citizens of the world: ask not what America will do for you, but what together we can do for the freedom of man."

SECRET #86:

Climax embedded in a repetitive template.

It's a shame that the frequent quotations of this speech include the previous passage but exclude this one, when this one is simply a rhetorical continuation of the previous one.

It's another climax; it escalates from the previous statement to a more intense, elevated plane of existence. And not only is it a climax, but it is a climax intensifying off a repetitive mold. It's first, "ask not what your country can do for you, but (statement)," and then "ask not what this country can do for you, but (more intensified statement)." The essentially repeated first halves of these two sentences give the climax more rhetorical force. And the final passage raises the intensity yet one more time, in a beautifully fitting way.

THE BASIC ONE-STEP RHETORICAL ALGORITHM

YOUR   ELOQUENCE   UPGRADED
MESSAGE   ALGORITHM   MESSAGE

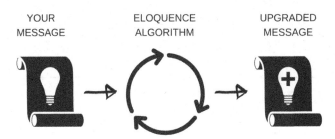

FIGURE 48: Remember how these strategies function as repeatable, plug-and-play algorithms for eloquence.

THE POWERFUL PROCESS YOU ARE NOW CAPABLE OF

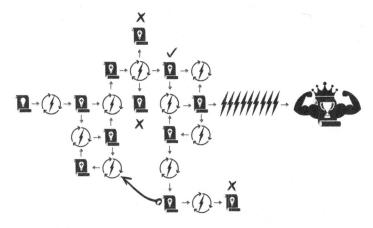

FIGURE 49: You know the algorithms. You are now capable of chaining them together, creating a message (or brushing up the clothing of a message) in such a way that it can stand along the legendary speeches of legendary leaders: words that changed the world.

A PERFECT EXAMPLE OF ALGORITHMIC CHAINING

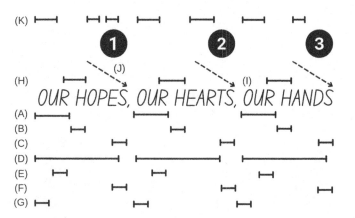

FIGURE 50: The rhetorical strategy of these six words includes repetition of inclusive pronouns (A), alliteration (B), reverse alliteration (C), parallelism (D), reverse alliteration (E), fragmented reverse alliteration (F),

fragmented alliteration (G), consonance (H), asyndeton (I), reverse climax (J), assonance (K), and tricolon.

COUNTERING THE RHYME AS REASON EFFECT

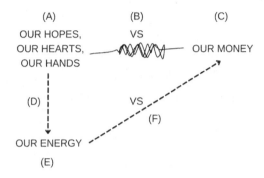

FIGURE 51: Evaluating an aesthetic message (A) produces biased thinking (B) when it competes against a message lacking aesthetic impact (C). This is the aesthetic impact bias, or the rhyme as reason effect. Overcome this by restating the aesthetic message (D) in the same style as the standard one (E) and comparing these versions (F).

PASSAGE #26:

Finally, whether you are citizens of America or citizens of the world, ask of us the same high standards of strength and sacrifice which we ask of you. With a good conscience our only sure reward, with history the final judge of our deeds, let us go forth to lead the land we love, asking His blessing and His help, but knowing that here on earth God's work must truly be our own.

...............................Chapter Summary................................

- JFK, like Clinton and Reagan, spoke with rhetorical continuity throughout the address.

- JFK's rhetorical continuity between passages is placed center-stage in a way that exceeds Clinton and Reagan.
- JFK used many of the same basic rhetorical building blocks as Reagan and Clinton (such as alliteration, parallelism, etc).
- JFK built particularly striking and unique rhetorical constructions, combining the same devices in new ways.
- JFK produced a compelling rhetorical climax by using deliberately designed language to create an intensity peak.
- JFK's most notable and unique strategy was (probably) creating a third metaphor out of two sub-metaphors.

KEY INSIGHT:

There Are Six Different Types of Chess Pieces. And Yet the Set of Permutations of Potential Chess Games is Virtually Infinite.

Rhetoric is Similar. A Finite Number of Devices Yields a World of Infinite Possibility.

YOUR RHETORICAL TOOLBOX (PART THREE)

1	Use Clinton's Rhetorical Secrets
1.1	Inclusive Pronouns Establish Empathy and Parity
1.2	Your Subject is What You're Talking About
1.3	Your Lens is the Perspective You Approach the Subject Through
1.4	Alliteration Starts Consecutive Words with the Same Sound
1.5	Alliterative Couples are Two Consecutive Alliterative Words
1.6	Fragmented Alliteration Has Intervening Words Breaking It Up
1.7	Reverse Alliteration Ends Words with the Same Sound
1.8	Tricolons are Lists of Three Creating Compelling Flow and Rhythm
1.9	Nested Rhetorical Devices Occur Within a Dominant Device
1.10	Opposing Structures, Meanings, Words, etc., Create Contrast
1.11	Matching Structures, Meanings, Words, etc., Create Symmetry
1.12	Superabundance is Rhetorical Addition; Expansion; Stretching
1.13	Intensifying Superabundance Adds a Pile of Intense Elaboration
1.14	"Verb-Saturated" Language Delivers Action-Oriented Narrative
1.15	Layered Devices Are of Equal Force and Occur Concurrently
1.16	In- and Out-Flow Occurs When One Word Ends Device A, Starts B
1.17	Fragmented Alliterative Couplets: "Strong and Stable."
1.18	Reverse Fragmented Alliteration: "Fight for What is Right."
1.19	Enumeratio Breaks Up an Item into its Constituent Parts

1.20	Assonance Repeats Vowel Sounds in Close Proximity
1.21	Consonance Repeats Consonant Sounds in Close Proximity
1.22	Parallelism Occurs When Segments Share Grammatical Structure
1.23	Loose Parallelism Occurs When Segments Only Share Grammar
1.24	Front-Back Alliteration: "Strong, Fast"
1.25	Phonetically Undone Couplet: Two Phonetics Undoing Each Other
1.26	Action-Oriented Language Creates a Self-Driven Narrative
1.27	Strict Parallelism is Identical Grammar and Some Word Repetition
1.28	Strictly Parallel Tricolon: Three Comma-Split Strict Parallels
1.29	Asyndeton Omits Grammatically Accurate Conjunctions
1.30	Pattern-Interrupts Break Away from a Preceding Pattern
1.31	Micro Devices Occur on Small Scales: Letters and Words
1.32	Macro Devices Occur on Large Scales: Paragraphs and Passages
1.33	X, X, YX Pattern-Interrupts: "From Time to Time... Our Time."
1.34	Simple Contrast: Two Contrasting Words in Close Proximity
1.35	Anaphora Starts Subsequent Sentences with the Same Words
1.36	Anaphora Paradigms are Anaphora-Based Structural Segments
1.37	Fragmented Anaphora Paradigms Have Intervening Material
1.38	X, YX Pattern-Interrupts: "It Can Be Done, and Done Fairly."
1.39	Stacked Pattern Interrupts Stack Pattern-Breaking Strategies

1.40	A, B1X, C1Y, D1Z Constructions: "For X, From X, To X"
1.41	Micro-Parallelism is Word or Segment-Level Parallelism
1.42	Stacked Micro-Parallelism Stacks Micro-Parallel Segments
1.43	Noun Couplets Emphasize an Item by Using Two Words for it
1.44	Stacked Contrasts Stack Contrasting Phrases Together
1.45	Symmetrical Word Choice Creates Rhetorical Unity
1.46	Inundating Contrasts Creates a "Superabundance" of Contrast
1.47	"While" Constructions Transition and Create Narrative Movement
1.48	Attached Adjectives Modify Directly Subsequent Nouns
1.49	Climax Arranges Items in Order of Increasing Intensity
1.50	Reverse Climax Arranges Items in Order of Decreasing Intensity
1.51	Letter-Level Flow: Rhetorical Symmetry at the Smallest Level
1.52	Tiered O-A Flow: A Particular Form of Letter-Level Flow
1.53	Themes Are Perspectives Through Which to View a Subject
1.54	Metaphors Equate Two Items
1.55	Theme-Indicating Metaphors Compare the Theme to Something
1.56	Rhetorical Emphasis Uses Components of Rhetoric to Emphasize
1.57	Periodic Sentences Place the Key Word in the Final Position
1.58	Stacked Periodic Segments Sequence Periodic Segments
1.59	Double Attached Adjectives: "America's Long Heroic Journey..."

2.18	Stacked Reverse Antitheticals: "X, Not Y, Not Z"
2.19	Sentence-Intervened Repetition: "The Price... Pay that Price"
2.20	NA1, YA2 Constructions: "Not A if 1... A if 2"
2.21	Conduplicatio Repeats a Word Across Segments, Sentences, etc.
2.22	A1, A2, A3, B1, B2, B3: "Our X, Our Y, Our Z; the X, the Y, the Z"
2.23	Anadiplosis: The Last Word of a Segment as the First of the Next
2.24	Loose Anadiplosis: Roughly the Last Word Repeated Roughly First
2.25	Enveloped Phonetic Repetition: "Our Country... Our Countrymen"
2.26	Hypophora: Asking and then Answering a Rhetorical Question
2.27	Open Loops Are Created by Triggered but Unanswered Curiosity
2.28	Hypophora-Based Open Loops Create the Loop with Hypophora
2.29	Borrowed Eloquence Uses Relevant, Eloquent Quotations
2.30	Personal Style is the Unique Aspects of an Individual's Language
2.31	Universal Themes Crop Up Over and Over Despite Personal Styles
2.32	Varied Sentence Lengths Create Intrigue and Maintain Attention
2.33	Stacked Anaphora Sequences Anaphora Paradigms
2.34	Floating Opposites: "Adjective A Noun B, Adjective -A Noun -B"
2.35	Sacred-Profane Spectrum: Everyday to Sanctified Language
2.36	Speaking to the Moment: Stating What is Happening "Now"
2.37	"VSDC" Verbs: Visual, Specific, Detail-Oriented, Concrete Verbs

2.38	Visually Stimulating Scenes Draw Listeners into a Mental Movie
2.39	A14, A24, A31: "A1 (1, 2, 3, 4), A2 (1, 2, 3, 4), A3 (1)"
2.40	Micro-Climax: Word-Level Rhetorical Climax
3	**Use JFK's Rhetorical Secrets**
3.1	Inclusive Greetings Begin by Acknowledging Every "Sub-Audience"
3.2	Grammatical Parallelism Mirrors Grammatical Structures
3.3	Strategic Connotation Optimizes the Implied Nuances of Words
3.4	Strict Parallelism is Perfect Grammatical Parallelism
3.5	Then-and-Now Constructions Contrast the Past with the Present
3.6	Crescendo Sentences is a Sequence of Lengthening Sentences
3.7	Structure-Meaning Alignment Uses Structure to Mirror Meaning
3.8	Auxiliary Words are Non-Substantive "Helper" Words
3.9	Meaningful Words are Substantive, Important Words
3.10	The Auxiliary-Substance Guidelines Define Their Treatment
3.11	Reducing Auxiliary Words Removes Diluting Auxiliaries
3.12	Bundling Auxiliary Words Places Auxiliary Words Together
3.13	Bundling Meaningful Words Places Meaningful Words Together
3.14	Placement-Based Emphasis is Created by Position in the Sentence
3.15	Rhetoric-Based Emphasis is Created by Rhetorical Devices
3.16	Formal Auxiliaries are Elevated Auxiliary Words: "Shall"

JFK'S SEQUENCED ANAPHORA PARADIGMS

A
Let the word go forth... **A1**
Let every nation know... **A2**

B
To those old allies... **B1**
To those new states... **B2**
To those people in the huts and villages.... **B3**
To our sister republics... **B4**
To that world assembly... **B5**
To those nations... **B6**

C
Let us begin anew... **C1**
Let us never negotiate out of fear... **C2**
Let us never fear to negotiate... **C3**

D
Let both sides explore... **D1**
Let both sides [...] formulate... **D2**
Let both sides seek... **D3**
Let both sides unite... **D4**
Let both sides join... **D5**

Claim These Free Resources that Will Help You Unleash the Power of Your Words and Speak with Confidence. Visit www.speakforsuccesshub.com/toolkit for Access.

18 Free PDF Resources

12 Iron Rules for Captivating Story, 21 Speeches that Changed the World, 341-Point Influence Checklist, 143 Persuasive Cognitive Biases, 17 Ways to Think On Your Feet, 18 Lies About Speaking Well, 137 Deadly Logical Fallacies, 12 Iron Rules For Captivating Slides, 371 Words that Persuade, 63 Truths of Speaking Well, 27 Laws of Empathy, 21 Secrets of Legendary Speeches, 19 Scripts that Persuade, 12 Iron Rules For Captivating Speech, 33 Laws of Charisma, 11 Influence Formulas, 219-Point Speech-Writing Checklist, 21 Eloquence Formulas

Claim These Free Resources that Will Help You Unleash the Power of Your Words and Speak with Confidence. Visit www.speakforsuccesshub.com/toolkit for Access.

30 Free Video Lessons

We'll send you one free video lesson every day for 30 days, written and recorded by Peter D. Andrei. Days 1-10 cover authenticity, the prerequisite to confidence and persuasive power. Days 11-20 cover building self-belief and defeating communication anxiety. Days 21-30 cover how to speak with impact and influence, ensuring your words change minds instead of falling flat. Authenticity, self-belief, and impact – this course helps you master three components of confidence, turning even the most high-stakes presentations from obstacles into opportunities.

Claim These Free Resources that Will Help You Unleash the Power of Your Words and Speak with Confidence. Visit www.speakforsuccesshub.com/toolkit for Access.

2 Free Workbooks

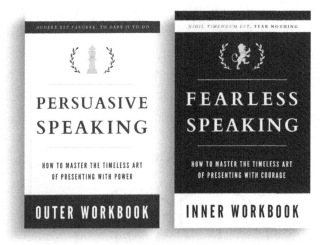

We'll send you two free workbooks, including long-lost excerpts by Dale Carnegie, the mega-bestselling author of *How to Win Friends and Influence People* (5,000,000 copies sold). *Fearless Speaking* guides you in the proven principles of mastering your inner game as a speaker. *Persuasive Speaking* guides you in the time-tested tactics of mastering your outer game by maximizing the power of your words. All of these resources complement the Speak for Success collection.

SOMETHING WAS MISSING. THIS IS IT.

D ECEMBER OF 2021, I COMPLETED the new editions of the 15 books in the Speak for Success collection, after months of work, and many 16-hour-long writing marathons. The collection is over 1,000,000 words long and includes over 1,700 handcrafted diagrams. It is *the* complete communication encyclopedia. But instead of feeling relieved and excited, I felt uneasy and anxious. Why? Well, I know now. After writing over 1,000,000 words on communication across 15 books, it slowly dawned on me that I had missed the most important set of ideas about good communication. What does it *really* mean to be a good speaker? This is my answer.

THERE ARE THREE DIMENSIONS OF SUCCESS

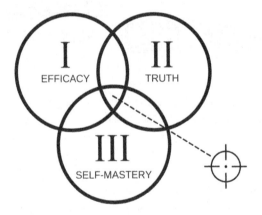

FIGURE I: A good speaker is not only rhetorically effective. They speak the truth, and they are students of self-mastery who experience peace, calm, and deep equanimity as they speak. These three domains are mutually reinforcing.

I realized I left out much about truth and self-mastery, focusing instead on the first domain. On page 33, the practical guide is devoted to domain I. On page 42, the ethical guide is devoted to domain II. We will shortly turn to domain III with an internal guide.

WHAT A GOOD SPEAKER LOOKS LIKE

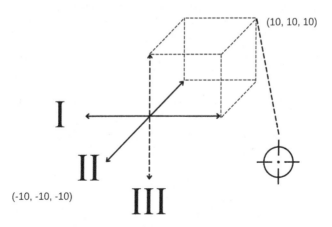

FIGURE II: We can conceptualize the three domains of success as an (X, Y, Z) coordinate plane, with each axis extending between -10 and 10. Your job is to become a (10, 10, 10). A (-10, 10, 10) speaks the truth and has attained self-mastery, but is deeply ineffective. A (10, -10, 10), speaks brilliantly and is at peace, but is somehow severely misleading others. A (10, 10, -10), speaks the truth well, but lives in an extremely negative inner state.

THE THREE AXES VIEWED DIFFERENTLY

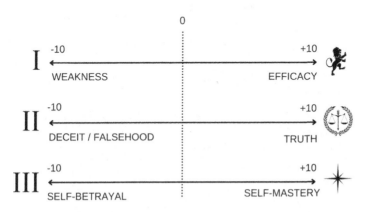

FIGURE III: We can also untangle the dimensions of improvement from representation as a coordinate plane, and instead lay them out flat, as spectrums of progress. A

(+10, -10, -10) is a true monster, eloquent but evil. A (10, 10, 10) is a Martin Luther King. A more realistic example is (4, -3, 0): This person is moderately persuasive, bends truth a little too much for comfort (but not horribly), and is mildly anxious about speaking but far from falling apart. Every speaker exists at some point along these axes.

THE EXTERNAL MASTERY PROCESS IS INTERNAL TOO

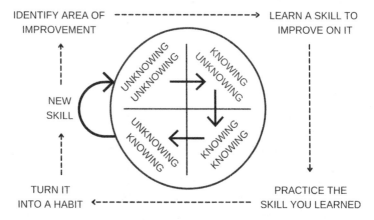

FIGURE IV: The same process presented earlier as a way to achieve rhetorical mastery will also help you achieve self-mastery. Just replace the word "skill" with "thought" or "thought-pattern," and the same cyclical method works.

THE THREE AXES, IN DIFFERENT WORDS

Domain One	Domain Two	Domain Three
Efficacy	Truth	Self-Mastery
Rhetoric	Research	Inner-Peace
Master of Words	Seeker of Truth	Captain of Your Soul
Aristotle's "Pathos"	Aristotle's "Logos"	Aristotle's "Ethos"
Impact	Insight	Integrity
Presence of Power	Proper Perspective	Power of Presence
Inter-Subjective	Objective	Subjective
Competency	Credibility	Character
External-Internal	External	Internal
Verbal Mastery	Subject Mastery	Mental Mastery
Behavioral	Cognitive	Emotional

THE POWER OF LANGUAGE

Language has generative power. This is why many creation stories include language as a primordial agent playing a crucial role in crafting reality. "In the beginning was the Word, and the Word was with God (John 1:1)."

Every problem we face has a story written about its future, whether explicit or implicit, conscious or subconscious. Generative language can rewrite a story that leads downward, turning it into one that aims us toward heaven, and then it can inspire us to realize this story. It can remove the cloud of ignorance from noble possibilities.

And this is good. You can orient your own future upward. That's certainly good for you. You can orient the future upward for yourself and for your family. That's better. And for your friends. That's better. And for your organization, your community, your city, and your country. That's better still. And for your enemies, and for people yet unborn; for all people, at all times, from now until the end of time.

And it doesn't get better than that.

Sound daunting? It is. It is the burden of human life. It is also the mechanism of moral progress. But start wherever you can, wherever you are. Start by acing your upcoming presentation.

But above all, remember this: all progress begins with truth.

Convey truth beautifully. And know thyself, so you can guard against your own proclivity for malevolence, and so you can strive toward self-mastery. Without self-mastery, it's hard, if not nearly impossible, to do the first part; to convey truth beautifully.

Truth, so you do good, not bad; impact, so people believe you; and self-mastery, as an essential precondition for truth and impact. Imagine what the world would be like if everyone were a triple-ten on our three axes. Imagine what good, what beauty, what bliss would define our existence. Imagine what good, what beauty, what bliss could define our existence, here and now.

It's up to you.

THE INNER GAME OF SPEAKING

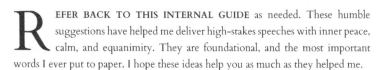

REFER BACK TO THIS INTERNAL GUIDE as needed. These humble suggestions have helped me deliver high-stakes speeches with inner peace, calm, and equanimity. They are foundational, and the most important words I ever put to paper. I hope these ideas help you as much as they helped me.

MASTER BOTH GAMES. Seek to master the outer game, but also the inner game. The self-mastery game comes before the word-mastery game, and even the world-mastery game. In fact, if you treat *any* game as a way to further your self-mastery, setting this as your "game above all games," you can never lose.

ADOPT THREE FOUNDATIONS. Humility: "The other people here probably know something I don't. They could probably teach me something. I could be overlooking something. I could be wrong. They have something to contribute" Passion: "Conveying truth accurately and convincingly is one of the most important things I'll ever do." Objectivity: "If I'm wrong, I change course. I am open to reason. I want to *be* right; I don't just want to seem right or convince others I am."

STRIVE FOR THESE SUPERLATIVES. Be the kindest, most compassionate, most honest, most attentive, most well-researched, and most confident in the room. Be the one who cares most, who most seeks to uplift others, who is most prepared, and who is most thoughtful about the reason and logic and evidence behind the claims.

START BY CULTIVATING THE HIGHEST VIRTUES IN YOURSELF: love for your audience, love for truth, humility, a deep and abiding desire to make the world a better place, the desire to both be heard and to hear, and the desire to both teach and learn. You will find peace, purpose, clarity, confidence, and persuasive power.

START BY AVOIDING THESE TEMPTING MOTIVES. Avoid the desire to "outsmart" people, to overwhelm and dominate with your rhetorical strength, to embarrass your detractors, to win on the basis of cleverness alone, and to use words to attain power for its own sake. Don't set personal victory as your goal. Strive to achieve a victory for truth. And if you discover you are wrong, change course.

LISTEN TO YOURSELF TALK. (Peterson, 2018). See if what you are saying makes you feel stronger, physically, or weaker. If it makes you feel weaker, stop saying it. Reformulate your speech until you feel the ground under you solidifying.

SPEAK FROM A PLACE OF LOVE. It beats speaking from a desire to dominate. Our motivation and purpose in persuasion must be love. It's ethical *and* effective.

LOVE YOUR ENEMIES (OR HAVE NONE). If people stand against you, do not inflame the situation with resentment or anger. It does no good, least of all for you.

AVOID THESE CORRUPTING EMOTIONS: resistance, resentment, and anger. Against them, set acceptance, forgiveness, and love for all, even your enemies.

PLACE YOUR ATTENTION HERE, NOW. Be where you are. Attend to the moment. Forget the past. Forget the future. Nothing is more important than this.

FOCUS ON YOURSELF, BUT NOW. Speaking gurus will tell you to focus solely on your audience. Yes, that works. But so does focusing on yourself, as long as you focus on yourself *now*. Let this focus root you in the present. Don't pursue a mental commentary on what you see. Instead, just watch. Here. Now. No judgment.

ACCEPT YOUR FEAR. Everyone fears something. If you fear speaking, don't fear your fear of speaking too. Don't reprimand yourself for it. Accept it. Embrace it, even. Courage isn't action without fear. Courage is action despite fear.

STARE DOWN YOUR FEAR. To diminish your fear, stare at the object of your fear (and the fear itself), the way a boxer faces off with his opponent before the fight. Hold it in your mind, signaling to your own psyche that you can face your fear.

CHIP AWAY AT YOUR FEAR. The path out of fear is to take small, voluntary steps toward what you fear. Gradual exposure dissolves fear as rain carves stone.

LET THE OUTER SHAPE THE INNER. Your thoughts impact your actions. But your actions also impact your thoughts. To control fear, seek to manage its outward manifestations, and your calm exterior will shape your interior accordingly.

KNOW THAT EGO IS THE ENEMY. Ego is a black storm cloud blocking the warm sunlight of your true self. Ego is the creation of a false self that masquerades as your true self and demands gratification (which often manifests as the destruction of something good). The allure of arrogance is the siren-song of every good speaker. With it comes pride and the pursuit of power; a placing of the outer game before the inner. Don't fall for the empty promises of ego-gratification. Humility is power.

DON'T IDENTIFY WITH YOUR POSITIONS. Don't turn your positions into your psychological possessions. Don't imbue them with a sense of self.

NOTICE TOXIC AVATARS. When person A speaks to person B, they often craft a false idea, a false avatar, of both themselves and their interlocuter: A1 and B1. So does person B: B2 and A2. The resulting communication is a dance of false avatars; A1, B1, B2, and A2 communicate, but not person A and B. A false idea of one's self speaks to a false idea of someone else, who then does the same. This may be why George Bernard Shaw said "the greatest problem in communication is the illusion that it has been accomplished." How do you avoid this dance of false avatars? This conversation between concepts but not people? Be present. Don't prematurely judge. Let go of your *sense* of self, for just a moment, so your real self can shine forth.

MINE THE RICHES OF YOUR MIND. Look for what you need within yourself; your strengths and virtues. But also acknowledge and make peace with your own capacity for malevolence. Don't zealously assume the purity of your own motives.

RISE ABOVE YOUR MIND. The ability to think critically, reason, self-analyze, and self-criticize is far more important than being able to communicate, write, and speak. Introspect before you extrospect. Do not identify as your mind, but as the awareness eternally watching your mind. Do not be in your mind, but above it.

CLEAR THE FOG FROM YOUR PSYCHE. Know what you believe. Know your failures. Know your successes. Know your weaknesses. Know your strengths. Know what you fear. Know what you seek. Know your mind. Know yourself. Know your capacity for malevolence and evil. Know your capacity for goodness and greatness. Don't hide any part of yourself from yourself. Don't even try.

KNOW YOUR LOGOS. In 500 B.C. Heraclitus defined Logos as "that universal principle which animates and rules the world." What is your Logos? Meditate on it. Sit with it. Hold it up to the light, as a jeweler does with a gem, examining all angles.

KNOW YOUR LIMITS. The more you delineate and define the actions you consider unethical, the more likely you are to resist when they seem expedient.

REMEMBER THAT EVERYTHING MATTERS. There is no insignificant job, duty, role, mission, or speech. Everything matters. Everything seeks to beat back chaos in some way and create order. A laundromat doesn't deal in clean clothes, nor a trash disposal contractor in clean streets. They deal in order. In civilization. In human dignity. Don't ignore the reservoir of meaning and mattering upon which you stand. And remember that it is there, no matter where you stand.

GIVE THE GIFT OF MEANING. The greatest gift you can give to an audience is the gift of meaning; the knowledge that they matter, that they are irreplaceable.

HONOR YOUR INHERITANCE. You are the heir to thousands of years of human moralizing. Our world is shaped by the words of long-dead philosophers, and the gifts they gave us: gems of wisdom, which strengthen us against the dread and chaos of the world. We stand atop the pillars of 4,000 years of myth and meaning. Our arguments and moral compasses are not like planks of driftwood in a raging sea, but branches nourished by an inestimably old tree. Don't forget it.

BE THE PERSON YOU WANT TO BE SEEN AS. How do you want to be seen by your audience? How can you actually be that way, rather than just seeming to be?

HAVE TRUE ETHOS. Ethos is the audience's perception that the speaker has their best interests at heart. It's your job to make sure this perception is accurate.

CHANGE PLACES WITH YOUR AUDIENCE. Put yourself in their shoes, and then be the speaker you would want to listen to, the speaker worthy of your trust.

ACT AS THOUGH THE WHOLE WORLD IS WATCHING. Or as though a newspaper will publish a record of your actions. Or as though you're writing your autobiography with every action, every word, and even every thought. (You are).

ACT WITH AUDACIOUS HONOR. As did John McCain when he called Obama, his political opponent, "a decent family man, [and] citizen, that I just happen to have disagreements with." As did Socrates and Galileo when they refused to betray truth.

ADOPT A MECHANIC'S MENTALITY. Face your challenges the way a mechanic faces a broken engine; not drowning in emotion, but with objectivity and clarity. Identify the problem. Analyze the problem. Determine the solution. Execute the solution. If it works, celebrate. If not, repeat the cycle. This is true for both your inner and outer worlds: your fear of speaking, for example, is a specific problem with a specific fix, as are your destructive external rhetorical habits.

APPLY THE MASTERY PROCESS INTERNALLY. The four-step mastery process is not only for mastering your rhetoric, but also for striving toward internal mastery.

MARSHAL YOURSELF ALONG THE THREE AXES. To marshal means to place in proper rank or position – as in marshaling the troops – and to bring together and order in the most effective way. It is a sort of preparation. It begins with taking complete stock of what is available. Then, you order it. So, marshal yourself along three axes: the rhetorical axis (your points, arguments, rhetorical techniques, key phrases, etc.), the internal axis (your peace of mind, your internal principles, your mental climate, etc.), and the truth axis (your research, your facts, your logic, etc.).

PRACTICE ONE PUNCH 10,000 TIMES. As the martial arts adage says, "I fear not the man who practiced 10,000 punches once, but the man who practiced one punch 10,000 times." So it is with speaking skills and rhetorical techniques.

MULTIPLY YOUR PREPARATION BY TEN. Do you need to read a manuscript ten times to memorize it? Aim to read it 100 times. Do you need to research for one hour to grasp the subject of your speech? Aim to research for ten.

REMEMBER THE HIGHEST PRINCIPLE OF COMMUNICATION: the connection between speaker and audience – here, now – in this moment, in this place.

KNOW THERE'S NO SUCH THING AS A "SPEECH." All good communication is just conversation, with varying degrees of formality heaped on top. It's all just connection between consciousnesses. Every "difference" is merely superficial.

SEE YOURSELF IN OTHERS. What are you, truly? Rene Descartes came close to an answer in 1637, when he said "cogito, ego sum," I think therefore I am. The answer this seems to suggest is that your thoughts are most truly you. But your thoughts (and your character) change all the time. Something that never changes, arguably even during deep sleep, is awareness. Awareness is also the precondition for thought. A computer performs operations on information, but we don't say the computer "thinks." Why? Because it lacks awareness. So, I believe what makes you "you," most fundamentally, is your awareness, your consciousness. And if you accept this claim – which is by no means a mystical or religious one – then you must also see yourself in others. Because while the contents of everyone's consciousness is different, the consciousness itself is identical. How could it be otherwise?

FORGIVE. Yourself. Your mistakes. Your detractors. The past. The future. All.

FREE YOUR MIND. Many of the most challenging obstacles we face are thoughts living in our own minds. Identify these thoughts, and treat them like weeds in a garden. Restore the pristine poise of your mind, and return to equanimity.

LET. Let what has been be and what will be be. Most importantly, let what is be what is. Work to do what good you can do, and accept the outcome.

FLOW. Wikipedia defines a flow state as such: "a flow state, also known colloquially as being in the zone, is the mental state in which a person performing some activity is fully immersed in a feeling of energized focus, full involvement, and enjoyment in the process of the activity. In essence, flow is characterized by the complete absorption in what one does, and a resulting transformation in one's sense of time." Speaking in a flow state transports you and your audience outside of space and time. When I entered deep flow states during my speeches and debates, audience members would tell me that "it felt like time stopped." It felt that way for me too. Speaking in a flow state is a form of meditation. And it both leads to and results from these guidelines. Adhering to them leads to flow, and flow helps you adhere to them.

MEDITATE. Meditation brings your attention to the "here and now." It creates flow. Practice silence meditation, sitting in still silence and focusing on the motions of your mind, but knowing yourself as the entity watching the mind, not the mind itself. Practice aiming meditation, centering your noble aim in your mind, and focusing on the resulting feelings. (Also, speaking in flow is its own meditation).

EMBARK ON THE GRAND ADVENTURE. Take a place wherever you are. Develop influence and impact. Improve your status. Take on responsibility. Develop capacity and ability. Do scary things. Dare to leap into a high-stakes speech with no preparation if you must. Dare to trust your instincts. Dare to strive. Dare to lead. Dare to speak the truth freely, no matter how brutal it is. Be bold. Risk failure. Throw out your notes. The greatest human actions – those that capture our hearts and minds – occur on the border between chaos and order, where someone is daring to act and taking a chance when they know they could fall off the tightrope with no net below. Training wheels kill the sense of adventure. Use them if you need to, but only to lose them as soon as you can. Speak from the heart and trust yourself. Put yourself out there. Let people see the gears turning in your mind, let them see you grappling with your message in real time, taking an exploration in the moment. This is not an automaton doing a routine. It's not robotic or mechanical. That's too much order. It's also not unstructured nonsense. That's too much chaos. There is a risk of failure, mitigated not by training wheels, but by preparation. It is not a perfectly practiced routine, but someone pushing themselves just beyond their comfort zone, right at the cutting-edge of what they are capable of. It's not prescriptive. It's not safe either. The possibility that you could falter and fall in real-time calls out the best from you, and is gripping for the audience. It is also a thrilling adventure. Have faith in yourself, faith that you will say the right words when you need to. Don't think ahead, or backward. Simply experience the moment.

BREAK THE SEVEN LAWS OF WEAKNESS. If your goal is weakness, follow these rules. Seek to control what you can't control. Seek praise and admiration from others. Bend the truth to achieve your goals. Treat people as instruments in your game. Only commit to outer goals, not inner goals. Seek power for its own sake. Let anger and dissatisfaction fuel you in your pursuits, and pursue them frantically.

FAIL. Losses lead to lessons. Lessons lead to wins. If there's no chance of failure in your present task, you aren't challenging yourself. And if you aren't challenging yourself, you aren't growing. And that's the deepest and most enduring failure.

DON'T BETRAY YOURSELF. To know the truth and not say the truth is to betray the truth and to betray yourself. To know the truth, seek the truth, love the truth, and to speak the truth and speak it well, with poise and precision and power… this is to honor the truth, and to honor yourself. The choice is yours.

FOLLOW YOUR INNER LIGHT. As the Roman emperor and stoic philosopher Marcus Aurelius wrote in his private journal, "If thou findest in human life anything better than justice, truth, temperance, fortitude, and, in a word, anything better than thy own mind's self-satisfaction in the things which it enables thee to do according to right reason, and in the condition that is assigned to thee without thy own choice; if, I say, thou seest anything better than this, turn to it with all thy soul, and enjoy that which thou hast found to be the best. But if nothing appears to be better than [this], give place to nothing else." And as Kant said, treat humans as ends, not means.

JUDGE THEIR JUDGMENT. People *are* thinking of you. They *are* judging you. But what is their judgment to you? Nothing. (Compared to your self-judgment).

BREAK LESSER RULES IN THE NAME OF HIGHER RULES. Our values and moral priorities nest in a hierarchy, where they exist in relation to one another. Some are more important than others. If life compels a tradeoff between two moral principles, as it often does, this means there is a right choice. Let go the lesser of the two.

DON'T AVOID CONFLICT. Necessary conflict avoided is an impending conflict exacerbated. Slay the hydra when it has two heads, not twenty.

SEE THE WHOLE BOARD. Become wise in the ways of the world, and learned in the games of power and privilege people have been playing for tens of thousands of years. See the status-struggles and dominance-shuffling around you. See the chess board. But then opt to play a different game; a more noble game. The game of self-mastery. The game that transcends all other games. The worthiest game.

SERVE SOMETHING. Everyone has a master. Everyone serves something. Freedom is not the absence of service. Freedom is the ability to choose your service. What, to you, is worth serving? With your work and with your words?

TAKE RESPONSIBILITY FOR YOUR RIPPLE EFFECT. If you interact with 1,000 people, and they each interact with 1,000 more who also do the same, you are three degrees away from one billion people. Remember that compassion is contagious.

ONLY SPEAK WHEN YOUR WORDS ARE BETTER THAN SILENCE. And only write when your words are better than a blank page.

KNOW THERE IS THAT WHICH YOU DON'T KNOW YOU DON'T KNOW. Of course, there's that you know you don't know too. Recognize the existence of both of these domains of knowledge, which are inaccessible to you in your present state.

REMEMBER THAT AS WITHIN, SO (IT APPEARS) WITHOUT. If you orient your aim toward goals fueled by emotions like insecurity, jealousy, or vengeance, the world manifests itself as a difficult warzone. If you orient your aim toward goals fueled by emotions like universal compassion and positive ambition, the beneficence of the world manifests itself to you. Your aim and your values alter your perception.

ORIENT YOUR AIM PROPERLY. Actions flow from thought. Actions flow from *motives*. If you orient your aim properly – if you aim at the greatest good for the greatest number, at acting forthrightly and honorably – then this motive will fuel right actions, subconsciously, automatically, and without any forethought.

STOP TRYING TO USE SPEECH TO GET WHAT YOU WANT. Try to articulate what you believe to be true as carefully as possible, and then accept the outcome.

LEARN THE MEANING OF WHAT YOU SAY. Don't assume you already know.

USE THE MOST POWERFUL "RHETORICAL" TACTIC. There is no rhetorical tool more powerful than the overwhelming moral force of the unvarnished truth.

INJECT YOUR EXPERIENCE INTO YOUR SPEECH. Speak of what you know and testify of what you have seen. Attach your philosophizing and persuading and arguing to something real, some story you lived through, something you've seen.

DETACH FROM OUTCOME. As Stoic philosopher Epictetus said: "There is only one way to happiness and that is to cease worrying about things which are beyond the power of our will. Make the best use of what is in your power, and take the rest as it happens. The essence of philosophy is that a man should so live that his happiness shall depend as little as possible on external things. Remember to conduct yourself in life as if at a banquet. As something being passed around comes to you, reach out your hand and take a moderate helping. Does it pass you? Don't stop it. It hasn't yet come? Don't burn in desire for it, but wait until it arrives in front of you."

FOCUS ON WHAT YOU CONTROL. As Epictetus said, "It's not what happens to you, but how you react to it that matters. You may be always victorious if you will never enter into any contest where the issue does not wholly depend upon yourself. Some things are in our control and others not. Things in our control are opinion, pursuit, desire, aversion, and, in a word, whatever are our own actions. Things not in our control are body, property, reputation, command, and, in one word, whatever are not our own actions. Men are disturbed not by things, but by the view which they take of them. God has entrusted me with myself. Do not with that all things will go well with you, but that you will go well with all things." Before a high-stakes speech or event, I always tell myself this: "All I want from this, all I aim at, is to conduct what I control, my thoughts and actions, to the best of my ability. Any external benefit I earn is merely a bonus."

VIEW YOURSELF AS A VESSEL. Conduct yourself as something through which truth, brilliantly articulated, flows into the world; not as a self-serving entity, but a conduit for something higher. Speak not for your glory, but for the glory of good.

Want to Talk? Email Me:

PANDREIBUSINESS@GMAIL.COM

This is My Personal Email.
I Read Every Message and
Respond in Under 12 Hours.

Made in the USA
Las Vegas, NV
06 January 2025

15708576R00157